DAILY DISCIPLINES
for the
CHRISTIAN MAN

PRACTICAL STEPS TO AN
EMPOWERED SPIRITUAL LIFE

DR. BOB BELTZ

NAVPRESS
BRINGING TRUTH TO LIFE
NavPress Publishing Group
P.O. Box 35001, Colorado Springs, Colorado 80935

The Navigators is an international Christian
organization. Jesus Christ gave His followers
the Great Commission to go and make
disciples (Matthew 28:19). The aim of The
Navigators is to help fulfill that commission by multiplying laborers for Christ in
every nation.

NavPress is the publishing ministry of The
Navigators. NavPress publications are tools
to help Christians grow. Although publications alone cannot make disciples or change
lives, they can help believers learn biblical
discipleship, and apply what they learn to
their lives and ministries.

© 1993 by Bob Beltz
All rights reserved. No part of this pub-
lication may be reproduced in any
form without written permission from
NavPress, P.O. Box 35001, Colorado
Springs, CO 80935.
Library of Congress Catalog Card Number:
93-86110
ISBN 08910-97651

The anecdotal illustrations in this book
are composites of real situations, and any
resemblance to people living or dead is
coincidental.

Unless otherwise identified, all Scripture
quotations in this publication are taken from
the *HOLY BIBLE: NEW INTERNATIONAL
VERSION*® (NIV®). Copyright © 1973, 1978,
1984, International Bible Society. Used by
permission of Zondervan Publishing House.
All rights reserved. Another version used is
the *King James Version*.

Printed in the United States of America

4 5 6 7 8 9 10 11 12 13 14 15/9 98 97 96 95

FOR A FREE CATALOG OF
NAVPRESS BOOKS & BIBLE STUDIES,
CALL 1-800-366-7788 (USA)
or 1-416-499-4615 (CANADA)

CONTENTS

To Richard Beach —
spiritual father, mentor, and lifelong friend

There is a friend who sticks closer than a brother.
(Proverbs 18:24)

ACKNOWLEDGMENTS

I would like to thank the many friends who helped make this book possible. To do so would actually be quite impossible in the brief space of this page. However, without the special help of a few men and women you would not be reading the ideas contained on these pages.

I am immensely grateful to Lois Curley, my agent, for everything she did to bring this project to publication. Many thanks to Karen Morrison, my administrative assistant, for all her help. *Mucho gracias* to the staff, elders, and members of Cherry Hills Community Church for their support and encouragement of my teaching ministry. *Merci* to Jim Dixon, my colleague in ministry for the last eighteen years, for all his support and encouragement. *Spaceba* to Dutch Franz and Kurt Unruh for technical assistance with the Mac. A huge *grazie* to Bill McCartney, Randy Phillips, and all the men at Promise Keepers who have sponsored this book. *Danke, danke, danke* to Don Oden for the gift of his artwork.

Finally, you have heard it said that behind every successful man you will find a surprised mother-in-law. I believe it would also be true to say that behind every godly man you will find a praying wife. *Toda raba* to my wife, Allison, and my children, Stephanie and Baker, for the role they play in my attempt to become God's man.

FOREWORD

If he's a typical American evangelical, even the best devotional literature just doesn't turn him on. It doesn't speak his language and talk about what's of interest to him — sports, for example. He knows that he needs spiritual stimulus and direction. Not only that, he really would appreciate help in becoming a stronger Christian. But so far he hasn't found a male-oriented guidebook that gives specific counsel, something that's the antithesis of stodgy preaching and yet clearly marks out the way faith can make a vital difference in everyday living.

Mr. Typical Evangelical (he has his counterparts everywhere in the world) is a Christian whose sincere belief in the gospel hasn't proved a transforming dynamic. He may be at least a moderately happy and successful member of the human family, yet in relationship to God his experience can be summed up as *drift, discouragement*, and *defeat*. But the help he needs to break through this spiritual bottleneck is available. Bob Beltz provides it with attention-jolting relevance.

What he does is take this soul-stultified disciple on a journey of *discovery* showing biblically the possibility of a God-relationship that is excitingly different. That discovery, as Beltz leads his now hopeful brother on step by step, arouses an urgent *desire*, a hunger and thirst for a vibrant God-relationship. And that *desire* motivates the *decision* to embark on a realistic *discipline* that produces change. Beltz doesn't blandly promise a thornless rose garden. He's aware that there's no infallible formula which, if casually followed, brings about change. He realizes that within and without, opposing forces will stymie spiritual progress unless they are overcome by prayerful diligence. Yet as a fellow-struggler who knows experientially the potentials as well as the difficulties of the faith-life, he charts a plan of action that will enable a drifting, discouraged, defeated son of God to become a liberated, growing "man in Christ" (2 Corinthians 12:2).

VERNON GROUNDS
CHANCELLOR, DENVER SEMINARY

INTRODUCTION
THE NEED FOR A PROGRAM

Mitch is dying. He is dying because certain habits he has not been able to master are killing him. Tragically, Mitch is not only dying physically; Mitch is also dying emotionally and spiritually. His behavior has reaped a destructive harvest. He has alienated himself from his wife and children; he has cut himself off from friends and business associates; he has even managed to shut down his own feelings. His name is really not important because his profile fits multitudes of men in our world today. Mitch is an alcoholic. He has a disease. It is killing him.

Ironically, Mitch has taken two major steps toward recovery from alcoholism. Several years ago he overcame the hurdle of denial and named his disease. Mitch knows and acknowledges that he is an alcoholic. Mitch also took a second step toward recovery. He became a member of Alcoholics Anonymous. "Hi, my name is Mitch. I am an alcoholic."

Every week Mitch faithfully attends AA meetings. He even manages to be sober when he attends. But often, in despair and with self-loathing, Mitch leaves his weekly meetings and heads for the bar. AA is not really helping Mitch. For several years he has not experienced the reality of recovery that other men in these same meetings are experiencing. Mitch is not getting better. He is getting worse! He is dying.

What is wrong with this picture? Why isn't Mitch getting better? After all, he has acknowledged his problem and is a member of AA. To an outsider, he might seem like an enigma. To an insider, the problem is immediately apparent. Mitch might be a member of AA, but he is not working the program. Joining AA is not the solution. Going to meetings is not the answer. The only way Mitch is going to get better is if he is willing to move beyond the recognition of the problem and begin to work the program. Only then will Mitch experience the power of recovery and save his life.

◊ ◊ ◊

Mike is dying, too. In some ways, not at all like Mitch; in other ways, exactly like him. Mike doesn't drink. As a matter of fact, for years he has held a certain judgmental and critical attitude toward those who drink, use drugs, overeat, or struggle with any number of addictive behaviors. Mike is actually very good at being judgmental and critical. He simply fails to recognize that his critical spirit is as much of an addictive behavior as Mitch's drinking. Mike needs to be critical for many of the same reasons that Mitch needs to drink. Mike is dying inside. He wants desperately to feel good about himself. His inner life is filled with a gnawing emptiness that drives him to behaviors that also isolate him from everyone in his life who could potentially bring him the love and joy he longs for.

Like Mitch, Mike has also named his disease. Several years ago Mike overcame the hurdle of denial and recognized that something was wrong with his life. He acknowledged a deep emptiness inside. He came to grips with his need for help. He reached out to God. Mike is a Christian in the authentic, biblical sense of the word. He has had the born-again experience which comes from repentance and reception of Jesus Christ as Lord and Savior. He has asked Christ to come into his life, and Christ has answered that prayer.

Mike joined a church and attends services every week. Like Mitch, he often barely makes it home from church before his self-defeating behaviors are in full swing. For several years Mike has lived with the self-knowledge that something is fundamentally (excuse the pun) wrong with his spiritual experience. He has heard of the transforming power of Jesus Christ. He has heard about the abundant life and fruitful living. But Mike is not experiencing it. Experientially, Christianity is not working for Mike. Why?

Mike actually has the same underlying problem as Mitch. An outsider might peg him as just another boring and hypocritical churchgoer: shades of the Church Lady from *Saturday Night Live*. But an insider knows exactly where the problem lies. Mike might be a Christian, but he is not working the program. Joining a church is not the solution. Going to church is not the answer. The only way Mike is going to move beyond the recognition of his problem and begin to experience personal recovery and the promised abundant life is to work the program.

THE TWELVE STEPS

For several years I have been intrigued by the phenomenon of Alcoholics Anonymous. Without any paid staff, buildings, advertising budgets, management consultants, or efficiency experts, AA has become one of the most successful movements in the world. From Manhattan to Moscow, on any day of the week, in virtually any city of the world, you can find a growing fellowship of men and women who are experiencing personal growth and recovery through the influence of AA.

Part of the phenomenal success of AA is to be found in the practical daily program they have developed. The twelve-step program of AA has been immensely successful, not only in helping recovering alcoholics, but also in its many modified forms in helping multitudes of men and women who struggle with a wide variety of life-diminishing difficulties. From eating disorders to sexual addictions, twelve-step programs help people live more productive lives and overcome the struggles that have made their lives dysfunctional.

My interest in the program prompted a friend to give me a copy of the "Big Book." It didn't take long to discover the reason for the immense success of AA. Every principle of the twelve-step program is biblical. Step by step, men and women in AA groups learn how to live in the way Jesus taught the disciples to live. The groups themselves are beautiful models of what New Testament fellowship was meant to be. The success of AA should be a challenging model for the church. What the church has often failed to do is to help its members develop a simple, practical, daily program for developing personal spiritual vitality.

K.I.S.S.

"Keep it simple, stupid!" Perhaps it's not a very flattering cliché, but it is one that most Christian men would like to direct at their pastors. I know, I am one—a pastor, that is. For over twenty years I have taught Bible studies at least twice a week. That means that I have delivered somewhere in the area of two thousand messages. Periodically I repeat myself, but after twenty years I am still developing new material, primarily because I have stuffed an enormous amount of information into my brain over those years.

I have information! I am the product of twenty-five years of education. I finished high school and college. I went on to graduate school. I have even earned a doctorate. I think it is safe to say that I have been educated beyond my intelligence! If information were the key to authentic spirituality, I would be Super-Christian. Unfortunately, the vast reservoir of biblical data contained within the funny gray matter inside my skull doesn't always seem to make a whole lot of difference in the quality of my spiritual experience. Don't get me wrong. I'm grateful for what I have learned and for those who have taught me. But when I analyze what I really need to know in order to walk with Christ with a sense of spiritual vitality on a daily basis, I realize that the information needed to accomplish the task is relatively simple. I don't even need twelve steps. I can usually get the job done in seven. All the other information is like icing on the cake. I enjoy it, but it simply reinforces the basics.

THE SEVEN STEPS

Because of my appreciation for the daily-program dimension of the twelve steps, I began to think through a way to take the most foundational operating principles of walking with Christ and develop them into a daily program for spiritual vitality. I wanted to be able to place in the hands of the men who sit under my teaching ministry a simple tool that would help them live one day at a time, with Christ, led by the Spirit.

I have discovered that strategies for spiritual living are critical. Several years ago I experienced a renaissance in my prayer life (see my book *Transforming Your Prayer Life*). After developing a successful approach to a more meaningful life of prayer, and after implementing it over a period of several years, I began to analyze what it takes to make positive changes in our daily spiritual experience. I concluded that change requires several dynamics:

Motivation. I believe that we do what we are motivated to do. I don't believe we do what we want to do, nor even that we always do what we know we need to do. I think we do what we are sufficiently motivated to do. I wanted to pray. I knew I needed a more significant prayer life. But it wasn't until I was adequately motivated to change in this area of my spiritual life that I actually took the necessary action that led to the change.

Decision. Motivation leads to decision. Again, we do what we really decide to do. The step of making a decision is a critical dynamic of change. When I fell in love with my wife, Allison, I began to have a desire to marry her, which grew into a motivation to marry her. But my motivation needed to be linked to a decision. Until I made the decision to get married, my motivation couldn't lead to the actual reality of marriage.

Strategy. Sometimes even motivation and decision are inadequate dynamics to lead to the desired change. If we do not know how to accomplish the change we are seeking, motivation and desire can produce great frustration. I believe this is often the case in our spiritual lives. We are frequently encouraged and exhorted to make certain changes. When the Holy Spirit works to convict us, we get the necessary motivation that leads us to the point of decision. But if we don't know how to change, our decision only produces frustration and defeat. What is needed is a strategy for actually accomplishing the change.

THE SEVEN STEPS—
A PREVIEW OF COMING ATTRACTIONS

Having realized this fact in relationship to prayer, I developed a strategy that worked in my life and could be taught to others. The response to this strategy was so positive that I began to think about how to design a daily program that provided a strategy for implementing the core dynamics of vital personal spirituality. The result is the program contained in these pages. If implemented, I believe it will transform your daily walk and keep you from ending up like Mitch and Mike.

Step One—Acknowledging Your Need
The seven steps begin with the recognition that without a bit of divine intervention in our lives, we are in big trouble. It seems ironic that what at first might feel like personal defeat is actually the beginning of moving into a greater experience of Christ's power and presence in our lives. In step one you will discover what I call the joy of powerlessness. Hopefully, you will understand why the spiritual journey has been so difficult and at times discouraging.

This step is the beginning of moving into a new daily experience of spiritual vitality and authenticity. When you fully understand the principles of step one, you will joyfully acknowledge that you can't do it! This will naturally lead you into the principles of steps two and three.

Step Two — Affirming God's Power

Having discovered the joy of powerlessness, you will then be ready to explore the reality of God's power. This is the secret of daily spiritual vitality. Jesus clearly instructed the disciples that "apart from me you can do nothing" (John 15:5). In this chapter you will learn how to apply the simple formula "I can't, He can!" You will see how the entire spiritual journey is rooted in what I consider the foundational theological principle of walking with Christ — justification by faith.

Steps one and two help us remember that our life in Christ is not a natural phenomenon. It is a supernatural phenomenon. From the moment of new birth until the instant we see Jesus face to face, the principle contained in step two will prepare us to tap into the power source of the daily walk.

Step Three — Tapping into the Power

Step three will introduce you to the person of the Holy Spirit. Have you ever thought that if Jesus were physically present with you, as He was with the disciples, you could live a more effective spiritual life? Do you know that you have a resource that even the disciples didn't have before Pentecost? He is called the Holy Spirit.

In step three you will not only learn about the Holy Spirit, you will actually discover how to allow Him to empower your life on a daily basis. This step will move you into the power dimension of the Christian life. You will now have an internal resource that will generate love, joy, peace, patience, kindness, goodness, faithfulness, gentleness, and self-control in and through your life.

Step Four — Maintaining Christ's Lordship

Step four will help you live more consistently in the power

of the Spirit. Even when we have tapped into the main resources of spiritual vitality, we will discover that obstacles exist that tend to throw us off track in our relationship with Jesus Christ. Step four will help you understand both the inner and outer worlds of the Spirit. You will learn how to use a simple tool called The Real-World Matrix. This tool will help you understand the reality of spiritual warfare and the challenges of living as God's man in a sinful world.

Step four will also teach you a new concept I call "flesh prevention." This tool will help you keep in step with the Spirit and conquer the defeating patterns of the old life. Finally, you will learn how to keep Christ in the lordship position in your life.

Step Five—Experiencing Spiritual Cleansing

What happens when you fail in your Christian life? Do you get discouraged? Do you feel like giving up? Do you carry around so much guilt and condemnation that you are spiritually immobilized? No more! Step five will help you understand the full implications of Jesus' death. Your appreciation for the work of the Cross will grow as you learn how to personally experience spiritual cleansing on a daily basis. You will be free from the guilt of past sin and ready to serve Christ in a new way.

Step five will teach you the skill of taking a personal spiritual inventory. It will help you identify personal areas of weakness for which you need an extra touch of Christ's power to overcome. This is the step that helps you get honest with God, yourself, and other people.

Step Six—Growing in Christ

A daily program that is effective in producing spiritual vitality will require developing the basic disciplines of

Christian growth. When used on a daily basis, these resources are designed to help you discover God's will for your life. This chapter will focus on giving you ideas about improving your relationship with God. It will help you understand how to grow in your knowledge of Christ and what to do in response to that knowledge.

Step Seven — Serving the Kingdom
The final step in your daily program will give you a strategy for moving into the world as a force for the Kingdom of God. Any approach to Christian spirituality that fails to move us into action is an inadequate program. All of the preceding steps are designed to prepare you to be a human vehicle through whom Jesus Christ lives His life. Mother Teresa once identified herself as a "pencil in the hand of God." She said it was God's job to do the thinking and writing. Her job was simply to be the vehicle He worked through. This is the great need of many men who have found their personal spirituality unfulfilling and stagnant. Step seven will give you a plan to become God's man, serving the Kingdom.

WORKING THE PROGRAM

The final chapter of this book is designed to help you take what each of the preceding chapters has taught and put it all together into a working whole that can be used on a daily basis. I have attempted to show you what it might look like when a man, much like you, actually begins to work the program.

If you are willing to take the time to carefully learn each step, and to make the effort to then put each step into action in a daily program, you can avoid the futile experience that both Mitch and Mike found to be so defeating.

You can begin to live the abundant life that Jesus promised. You can begin to become God's man.

Let me ask you an important question: What do you want? Are you satisfied with the status quo? If so, there is really no reason to read further. This is not a program for the status quo. But if what you want is a vital spiritual life that works on a daily basis, then I encourage you to get ready to move out and take step one.

CHECKPOINTS

Personal Reflection
1. What about Mitch's and Mike's struggle is most like your life?
2. Do you have a personal program that you know how to work?
3. What would you like to see change in your relationship with Christ?

Group Discussion
1. Share with the group your answers to the above questions.
2. How could you help each other work the program?
3. What thought in chapter 1 meant the most to you?

1
STEP ONE
ACKNOWLEDGING OUR NEED
Apart from me you can do nothing.
(John 15:5)

*Father, I am spiritually powerless, and apart
from Your divine intervention in my life
I do not have the ability to be Your man.*

I was having a rotten day. I guess we all have them occasionally. This one had been particularly bad. I don't remember the events of the day that had produced my frustration, but I vividly remember feeling extremely defeated by my response to the circumstances. Don't get me wrong. I hadn't been caught with a prostitute. I hadn't abused my wife or my children. I hadn't done anything outwardly that would have provided an adequate rationale for why I was so frustrated. But frustrated I was!

It was about four in the afternoon and I was trying to recover from the day by taking a hard walk. I have reached that point in my life where running takes too great a toll on my aging body, so I have given up jogging and started power walking instead. On this particular afternoon I was thinking about the frustration of my day as I hit full stride. Suddenly, my thoughts began to synchronize with each step I took. All of my struggle seemed to reduce itself into two simple words: *I can't.* I found myself repeating these two words to the rhythm of my steps. Inside my brain it sounded something like this: "I can't, I can't, I can't, I can't, I can't, I can't, I can't." There was a cadence to my thinking that was in perfect rhythm with my walk.

Something was actually quite therapeutic about this process. It brought me into harmony with the reality of my spiritual life. *I can't.* I believe this is the point of departure for all authentic spiritual experience. Authentic spiritual vitality begins with the paradox of powerlessness. In and of myself, I am spiritually powerless. In the realm of spiritual fundamentals, it doesn't get more basic than this.

THE FOUNDATIONAL THEOLOGICAL PRINCIPLE

My walking experience was actually quite theologically correct. Had anyone been able to hear the message repeating inside my cranium that afternoon, I'm sure they would have thought I was a bit off my rocker. However, I was simply affirming the underlying theological truth of all authentic, biblical spirituality.

If our daily spiritual walk is going to be both effective and authentic, it must be rooted in the revealed truth of God's Word. If there is a logical starting point in learning the Christian walk, it must have as its basis what I consider the foundational theological principle of all authentic, biblical spirituality. This principle has historically been called justification by faith.

Justification is a theological concept concerning man's relationship with God. The basic spiritual issue in life is how to have a proper relationship with God. The Apostle Paul borrowed a concept from the law courts of the first century to illustrate this foundational principle. To be justified meant to be declared righteous. To be righteous

meant to be in the right relationship with an acknowledged standard.

In a court of law, the law itself was the standard.
When a man was accused of violating the law, he stood
trial to determine whether or not he was guilty of the
accused violation. If the man's behavior did not measure up to the standard of the law, he was found to be
unrighteous—that is, not in conformity with the standard. If, on the other hand, the trial revealed that the man
had not violated but had in fact lived in conformity to
the standard, then the verdict was a declaration of the
person's rightness or righteousness. In this case, the man
was said to have been justified.

This historic situation provided an analogy for Paul
of the relationship between God and man. The standard
of rightness in relationship to God is the character of God
Himself. The issue becomes the ability of men to live up
to this standard. If performance matches the standard,
the verdict will be one of declared rightness. If performance does not meet the standard, then the man in question has a problem. He is unright or unrighteous as evaluated against the standard.

There are three possibilities that grow out of this scenario concerning a man's relationship with God. For the
sake of our discussion, let me identify them as plans A,
B, and C.

Plan A

Plan A is based on the assumption that I have the ability to
do something that will enable me to be found in the right
relationship with God. The classic illustration of this plan
would be Judaism at the time of Christ. Although it can
be demonstrated biblically that God never intended the
Old Testament Law to be a source of self-justification,

by the first century AD that is exactly how it was being used. Judaism taught that God's favor could be earned by keeping the Law. This plan has a major flaw: it can never work. Only one person in all of human history was able to live in a way that perfectly met the requirements of the Law in attitude, action, and intent. His name was Jesus, and He didn't need to earn God's favor. Plan A leads to either intense frustration or immense self-deception.

Plan B

Plan B begins with the premise that plan A won't work. Therefore, if there is nothing I can do to be in right relationship with God, and if in fact I am not in right relationship with God, then my only hope is that someone else can do something for me that will get me into a right relationship with God. If such a plan were possible, it would certainly be good news. Guess what? This is the message of the gospel! What I could never do, Jesus did for me. God has initiated a plan that enables me to have a relationship with Him based on what Christ has done. This plan is referred to as justification by faith. The plan is rooted in the grace and mercy of God. It is made possible by what Jesus accomplished on the cross.

If I am willing to come to God empty-handed and acknowledge my need; and if I am willing to personally respond to Jesus Christ by accepting His atonement as payment for my sin, embracing and receiving Him as my personal Savior and Lord; then God has promised that He will declare me right in His eyes as a gift of grace (Ephesians 2:8-9). This declaration of rightness is the meaning of the phrase *to justify*. Faith is my response to my own inability and Christ's finished work. I can be justified by faith!

Most of you reading this book have probably already

come to a point of personally receiving Jesus Christ as Lord and Savior. If not, and you would like to, then I encourage you to pray this prayer:

> Lord Jesus, I really need You. I don't have the ability to earn my way to You. I have sinned. I thank You that You died on the cross for me. I now turn to You and ask You to come into my life as Lord and Savior. I want to begin to live for You. Help me become the man You want me to be.

If you just prayed that prayer, or if you have ever sincerely prayed a prayer including the same basic elements, then you are in a right relationship with God on the basis of plan B. Plan B is rooted in grace, not performance. Plan A is a performance plan that does not work!

Plan C

In reality these are the only two alternatives for beginning a relationship with God. Some sects historically have argued for a plan C that combines the two. Plan C attempts to mix faith in Christ with a system of human works designed to somehow earn God's favor. Plan C is actually nothing more than plan A disguised. When Paul wrote his letter to the Galatian believers, he spoke of a gospel that was no gospel at all (Galatians 1:7). If we have to perform to be in relationship with God, there is no good news and we are in big trouble!

Here is the point of this theological discourse: the foundational theological principle of all authentic biblical spirituality is the principle of justification by faith. It is a theological principle clearly taught in the Bible. At its core is the revealed truth of human inability. You begin the entire Christian experience with a recognition of your powerlessness. You can only come to the party if you come empty-handed. Justification by faith affirms the truth of the "I can't" experience.

THE JOY OF POWERLESSNESS

When we trust Christ as the source of personal forgiveness and righteousness (right relationship with God), we begin a spiritual journey. On this journey we are intended to experience the freedom of coming to God on His terms, which do not include our performance. For many men this good start is followed by years of frustration trying to live the spiritual life. Why? I believe it is because part of our psychic makeup is hopelessly religious. "Religion" is all about my efforts to please God. Authentic spirituality is all about my freely given, freely received relationship with God through Christ.

Just as I have no ability in myself to enter into a relationship with God, I have discovered that I have no ability in my own strength to live daily in any way resembling what Jesus called an "abundant life" (John 10:10). Sometimes it takes years to discover this second phase of our own inability. When we discover it, it can be as liberating an experience as discovering the free gift of salvation.

I am spiritually powerless. I was powerless when I began the spiritual journey; I am powerless to live the journey day by day. I am powerless over the effects of the years of my separation from God and the impact those years had on my development as a man. Only God's grace provided the gift I needed to receive Christ. Only God's grace will enable me to live with His power in the midst of my powerlessness.

One night Jesus met with His disciples in an upper room in Jerusalem. It was the most important of many nights He had spent with them over the course of three years. This was the night before He would hang on a cross to pay the penalty for the sins of humanity and make it possible for powerless people to know, love, and serve God. In the upper room, Jesus gave the disciples His final instructions before He went to the cross.

The Apostle John's account of this night tells that Jesus used an illustration of a vine and its branches to teach the most important lesson He could teach about spiritual living. Jesus told the disciples that He was the vine and they were the branches. He taught them that apart from Him they could do nothing (John 15:5). The message of the illustration was one of their (and our) powerlessness and His empowerment. He went on to tell them that if they would abide in Him as a branch abides in the vine, they would bear much fruit. Fruit is a symbol of all Jesus wants to do in and through us. Fruitfulness is an image of vital living.

We all realize that there are many things we can do apart from Christ. But when it comes to effectively living the Christian life, all our efforts apart from His indwelling and empowerment are nothing. We are powerless.

At first glance this truth seems to be a bit depressing. After all, who wants to be powerless? Paradoxically, the more you understand this truth, the more liberated you will become, and the more prepared you will be to tap into the source of real power that makes spiritual vitality possible. I call this experience the joy of powerlessness. The pressure is off! I no longer have to struggle to try to do that which I cannot, or never could, do.

The joy of powerlessness is also the point of Jesus' first statement in the Sermon on the Mount. This discourse contains a brief synopsis of the keys to living a life of blessing. Jesus began the message with the declaration,

"Blessed are the poor in spirit" (Matthew 5:6). Since the word *poor* here is the Greek word *ptochos*, meaning "abject poverty," we could paraphrase this statement, "Blessed are the spiritually bankrupt." In other words, blessed are the powerless. Poverty of spirit comes from the recognition that I am totally dependent upon Christ not only to save me, but to enable me to live in a way that produces a life of blessing.

Recently, I had a life-changing experience. I took a few weeks off from work and with the blessing of my family went to live on an island in Puget Sound. I spent twenty-one days in a guided experience of solitude and prayer. I had no television, no radio, no magazines, no mail, no telephone, no books—not even a newspaper. All the normal sources of distraction were removed to help this be a time when I could hear God speak. During this time I was allowed to write in a journal. After these weeks I began to write my interactions with God in dialogue form. Don't get me wrong. I know how careful we have to be in evaluating what we think God might be saying to us. I simply was writing down how I thought God might verbally respond to the issues I was praying about.

When I came home I found myself periodically using this approach in my time alone with God.

I thought you might profit from seeing what this approach looked like on a day when I was clearly aware of my spiritual bankruptcy:

BOB: "Father, I am absolutely helpless."
GOD: "Exactly!"
BOB: "I don't have the ability to:
Love you
Love Allison
Be a good father to Stephanie and Baker

> Keep a job
> Manage our finances
> Have fun
> Not be a jerk
> Live effectively
> Be fruitful
> Contribute to humanity or the Kingdom
> Do anything."

GOD: "Correct!"

As bleak as this dialogue at first appears, complete spiritual bankruptcy is actually the first step toward experiencing a life of blessing. The good news proclaims that Jesus is more than ready to begin to live His life through us once we understand and acknowledge that we can't do it apart from Him. This truth frees us from the treadmill of trying and prepares us for moving forward in authentic spiritual empowerment.

APPLYING STEP ONE

By now I hope you have identified your own powerlessness. If so, you might be wondering how to use this truth in your daily walk. To begin using the seven steps of this book, acknowledge your powerlessness and rest in it on a daily basis. I begin working the program by praying something like this:

> Dear Father, I come to You today to acknowledge that I am powerless. I am fundamentally power-less — period! I am also powerless over the effects of my separation from You. Apart from Your inter-vention in my life today, I do not have the ability to be Your man.

It might seem simple, but that is the first step. With that prayer you have just cleared the decks of all futile self-effort and positioned yourself to tap into a power source that makes it possible for you to live a fruitful life in dynamic relationship with God.

CHECKPOINTS

Personal Reflection
1. Have you found the Christian life to be frustrating?
2. Which plan, A, B, or C, have you been on?
3. What areas of your life most reveal your powerlessness?

Group Discussion
1. Explain which part of the Christian life has been difficult for you.
2. Share when you were justified by faith.
3. How do you feel about the idea of being powerless?

2
Step Two
Affirming God's Power

I can do everything through him who gives me strength.
(Philippians 4:13)

Father, You are all-powerful. Only You have
the ability to enable me to become Your man.

"I can't!" This acknowledgment is the beginning of an exciting spiritual journey. However, if these two words expressed the only reality of my daily walk, I would be in big trouble. It probably doesn't take much imagination for most of us to identify with the frustration I spoke of in the last chapter. Remember my walking experience? If my whole walk had been executed to the rhythm of "I can't, I can't, I can't, I can't," I would have ended that walk just as frustrated as when I started it, even though I had just identified the first principle of living a vital, dynamic, spiritual life. It was the next two words that set me free.

After walking for a while in the "I can't" mode, I made a very subtle transition. Once the truth of my powerlessness set in, I was ready to begin to affirm the greatest truth in all of the universe. My powerlessness, and the recognition of that powerlessness, led me to an affirmation of Christ's power. Suddenly, I began to find myself repeating, "He can, He can, He can, He can, He can, He can, He can!" This is the flip side of powerlessness. I might be powerless, but Christ is all-powerful. He is the source of all power in the Christian life.

THE GREAT EXCHANGE

I am a machine nut! I love mechanical things that have wheels on them and transport people at high velocity. In other words, cars and motorcycles. This is a bad passion to have when you've been called to the ministry. In all probability you will never have the economic ability to indulge your passion. I had this passion long before I became a Christian.

In high school my car was my pride and joy. Back in those days most of my high school buddies longed to drive Corvettes. I was a little strange. I had a passion for Porsches. I even developed a strategy for owning one. I decided that when I went away to college I would try to buy a Volkswagen. I had saved money for college, and when I found out that I had received a scholarship I began to have visions of using my saved money to buy a new car. I remember driving away from the car dealer's lot in a brand-new, shiny, red VW bug. The year was 1968. I stuck a peace sign in the rear window and installed an awesome stereo system. I can't begin to tell you how totally cool this was in 1968! But the VW was only the first phase of my Porsche-acquisition program.

I planned on going to law school after college. I began to scheme about trading my VW the first year of law school for a Karmanghia convertible. This was the next step toward the Porsche. Then, once I made it through grad school and started working in a law firm, I would buy a Porsche. This was the plan. Fortunately, it never worked.

My Porsche-acquisition plan was interrupted my junior year in college by a very unexpected and welcome intrusion in my life: Jesus Christ. I became a Christian and began seeking God's will for my life. I never made it to law school. I graduated from the university and took a job as a youth minister in a small town in the Midwest. I was making $400 a month and my Porsche plan looked pretty bleak. Somewhere during those years as a youth pastor I prayed that the Lord would take my car passion away from me. He didn't. I continued to drive VWs for the next eight years.

In 1980 I came up with an idea about how I could afford to drive a Porsche. For several years I had been buying cars and fixing them up as a hobby. I developed a certain skill in buying and selling. One day it dawned on me: why not buy and sell *Porsches*, and drive them while I'm fixing them up? That year I bought my first Porsche. That was seventeen Porsches ago! I have owned almost every type of Porsche ever made, except for what I consider to be the ultimate Porsche: the 930 Turbo. The 930 is one of the few cars in the world that can give you whiplash without being hit by another vehicle. The power of this automobile is almost beyond comprehension.

Suppose that you know about my love of Porsches and especially my longing to someday own a 930 Turbo. Now imagine that one day I called you on the phone and told you that I had just acquired a 930 and wanted to bring it over to show you. Even if you could care less about my car fetish, you would probably be polite enough to invite me over.

Let's say you live about a mile away. I tell you I am on my way. We hang up the phone and you expect, any moment, to see me scream into your driveway. The minutes go by and I don't arrive. The hours go by and I still don't arrive. Just when you are about to phone the police and ask for an all-points bulletin to be issued, you look out the window and here I come—pushing the Porsche into your driveway. I am covered with dirt and grease. I am soaked through with sweat. But there is still an immense grin on my face! I ask you how you like my 930 and you ask me what's wrong with it. I tell you nothing is wrong. You ask me why I am pushing the car. I respond by asking you how else you think I could get it to your house from mine. You tell me I could start the engine and drive it over. I say, "Engine? What's an engine?"

You would think I was pretty foolish if this happened. Here I am using my own limited energy to push a $99,000 car that has over 400 horsepower. As silly as this story seems, that is exactly what many people are trying to do in their spiritual lives. They either don't know about the "engine," or they don't know how to turn it on.

The great exchange is the basis of all authentic biblical spirituality. Not only has Christ taken away my sin and declared me to be right in God's sight, He has come to dwell in my inner being. My heart has become Christ's home. Now, all the power that Christ possesses dwells in me, and "He can!" It is the indwelling presence of Jesus Christ that is the power source enabling me to live the Christian life.

THE WAY OF LIFE

There are two fundamental issues relating to Christian spirituality. One was addressed in the previous chapter: the basis of human righteousness in relationship to the living God. The other is an issue of life. I am not only powerless apart from Christ, I am actually dead. One microsecond before I received Jesus Christ as my personal Lord and Savior I had a very serious problem.

Human beings are born dead. I know that sounds like a contradiction, but it is true. When God created man He created him to have two distinct types of life. He made us physical beings who possessed organic life by virtue of our physical existence. Genesis 2:7 tells us that God formed man (physically) from the dust of the earth. This same text tells us that God breathed His own breath into the man and Adam became a living soul. The breath of God in the Bible is used synonymously with the concept of the Spirit of God. The two Hebrew words for "breath" and "spirit" are even used interchangeably. At the point of creation, Adam possessed the Spirit of God, endowing him with spiritual life as well as physical life.

The Hebrew word for life in Genesis is the plural *chaiyim*, hinting at the dual nature of human existence. In the New Testament this reality is much clearer. There are actually two different Greek words used to communicate the difference between physical and spiritual life. In the tenth chapter of John, Jesus tells the disciples that He came that they might have life (John 10:10). The word translated as "life" in this verse is the Greek word *zoe*. This is the word used most frequently to communicate the concept of spiritual life. In the very next verse, Jesus tells the disciples what it is going to cost Him to give them this spiritual life. He says He is going to lay down His life for them (John 10:11). Here the Greek word *psuche* is used. This word often was used to speak of physical life, even though many times it was used to refer to the human soul also.

God told Adam not to eat from the Tree of the Knowledge of Good and Evil. He warned Adam that if he did he would die (Genesis 2:17). Literally, the Hebrew text reads, "Dying, you will die." In the instant that Adam used his freedom to violate God's command, something horrible happened. Adam didn't fall on the ground and die physically. This would come. Immediately, his relationship with God was distorted. He became afraid of God and hid from Him. When confronted about his sin, Adam rationalized and blamed it on Eve. What happened? Adam lost something that God had imparted in the act of creation. Adam died spiritually as the Spirit of God was withdrawn because of his sin.

What was true of Adam in that instant is true of every man born on the planet. We are born physically alive, but spiritually dead. We need life. The Apostle Paul reminded the believers in Ephesus that before receiving Christ they had been "dead in [their] transgressions and sins" (Ephesians 2:1). He also told the believers in Rome that "the wages of sin is death" (Romans 6:23).

When Jesus Christ lived among us, He constantly was talking about this issue of life (*zoe*). One night a man by the name of Nicodemus came to visit Him. He told Jesus that even though he was a leader of the Jews and a teacher himself, he recognized that Jesus was a teacher sent from God. Jesus told Nicodemus that unless he was born again he could never enter the Kingdom of God. Jesus went on to explain that what is born of the flesh (physical birth) is flesh (physical), but only that which is born of the Spirit (spiritual birth) is spirit (John 3:3-6).

The second great problem of humanity is this issue of how to experience spiritual life. There is only one source of spiritual life. The Bible says, referring to Jesus, that "in him was life" (John 1:4). He is the source of a power that can overcome my powerlessness. I can't because I am dead. I need life. Jesus Christ gives life. The great exchange takes place at the moment I accept on my behalf what Jesus has done for me by dying on the cross and rising from the dead. In that moment I am forgiven and declared righteous. In that same instant, as I open my life to Christ and invite Him to come in, He sends the Holy Spirit to indwell my inner being. The Holy Spirit is the agent by which Jesus comes to live in me, and when the Spirit comes He brings life. I experience a second birth—a spiritual birth. Now the Spirit lives in me, and by His presence Jesus lives in me and has the ability to live through me. This transaction is illustrated by the following diagram:

BEFORE   AFTER

Christ *in* me is the source of power that makes the Christian life possible. Only one person in all of human history has ever lived the Christian life. His name was Jesus. Only one person in all of history still has the ability to live the Christian life. His name is still Jesus. The miracle of the Christian life is found in the amazing and miraculous fact that Jesus Christ chooses to live His life *through* us! He has come to indwell my being and work in and through my personality. I can't, but He can! This is the secret of living an effective and fruitful spiritual life.

APPLYING STEP TWO

In order to apply step two you need simply to ask Jesus Christ to live His life in and through you today. In prayer you might say something like this:

> Lord Jesus, I am powerless. I have no ability in myself, apart from Your intervention in my life, to live my life in a way that is pleasing to You. I acknowledge that "I can't." But, I believe in You, Lord. I believe that You are the source of all power. I invite You to live Your life in and through me today. Thank You that I can trust You to bring Your power into my life. Make me the kind of man You created me to be.

Once you have asked Christ to begin to live in and through you, you are ready to learn how to continue to stay plugged into Him as the source of spiritual empowerment and fruitfulness. The agent through whom Christ indwells and empowers the life of a man who belongs to Him is the Holy Spirit. Understanding how to stay empowered by the Spirit is the lesson we need to learn when we take step three.

CHECKPOINTS

Personal Reflection
1. How much of your struggle to be God's man is a product of self-effort?
2. When did you ask Jesus Christ to live in you?
3. What areas of your life are in need of Christ's empowerment?

Group Discussion
1. Share your answers to the above questions.
2. Share a time when Christ gave you help to do something you could not do on your own.
3. In what areas of your life do you find it most difficult to rely on Christ?

3
STEP THREE
TAPPING INTO THE POWER
Be filled with the Spirit.
(Ephesians 5:18)

*Holy Spirit, I need You to fill my life today
with Your presence and power. Live the life of Christ
in and through me today.*

One of the greatest science fiction classics of cinematic history is a movie entitled *Invasion of the Body Snatchers*. It is such a classic that it has been remade several times to capture fresh audiences in new generations. The thesis of the movie is relatively simple: aliens are invading our planet and taking over the bodies of human beings. The process of invasion involves a period of time when the invaded human is encased in a cocoonlike membrane while the transformation of the alien personality occurs internally. Because of this process those humans who have been invaded are known in the movie as "pod people."

I bet you are wondering what all this has to do with being God's man. This movie provides an offbeat metaphor of what it takes to have a dynamic and effective daily walk with Christ. Authentic, biblical Christians have a great deal in common with the pod people. We are men who have been invaded by an "alien" life-form. One day we finally understood who Jesus Christ is and what the invitation to receive Him involves. We responded to an invitation to open the door of our lives and ask Christ to come in. When we extended that invitation to Jesus, our lives were invaded. Jesus Christ came to live in us.

THE PERSON OF THE HOLY SPIRIT

It is relatively easy to make the affirmation that we have received Jesus as our personal Lord and Savior. It is a bit tougher to explain exactly how Jesus Christ lives in us. After the Resurrection, Jesus appeared to the disciples in a flesh-and-bones body. They touched Him, talked with Him, and even had breakfast with Him (John 21:12). For forty days Jesus went to great lengths to make sure the fact was clear that His resurrection was a real, tangible, physical event.

In the first chapter of Acts, Luke records the event theologians call the Ascension. In the presence of the disciples, Jesus Christ physically lifted off the planet and returned to the throne of the Father in Heaven. This was not a mythological event. It was a very real physical event. His body physically rose until it disappeared from their sight. The message of the angels to the dumfounded disciples was that Jesus would come again in just the same way (Acts 1:11). The second coming of Jesus Christ will not be a mystical, esoteric, spiritual event. Jesus will return again occupying a real body. From the time of the Ascension until the time of the return, Jesus lives in bodily form in the presence of the Father (Colossians 2:9). Since this is the case, how can He come into our lives and dwell in our hearts?

One day the disciples became upset when Jesus told them that He was going to leave them. Jesus responded to their dismay by informing them that it was actually to their benefit for Him to leave. As long as He remained on earth, He was limited in His ability to be with them. He told them that when He returned to the Father and the place of glory He held from eternity past, He was going to send the person of the Holy Spirit to be with them forever. Even though the Spirit had been *with* them, He would now be *in* them (John 14:17). To understand how exciting that statement is, we need to know two important facts about the Holy Spirit.

Fact One — He Is Not an It!

The first fact we need to know is that the Holy Spirit is a person. I am constantly amazed at how loosely the Holy Spirit is defined these days. Many people pass the Spirit off as some kind of ethereal force or substance. The Bible is quite clear that the Spirit is a person. He is a who, not a what! He is a spiritual person.

Personality is a function of three primary capacities. The first is intellect. A force does not possess intellectual or rational capability. The Holy Spirit possesses intellect. We are told that He knows the mind of God (1 Corinthians 2:11).

The second component of personality is emotion. Again, a substance or force does not have the capacity to experience emotional responses. The Holy Spirit does. It is possible to grieve or cause emotional distress to the Spirit (Ephesians 4:30).

The final characteristic of personality is will or volition. Personality has the ability to make choices. The Holy Spirit is the agent who imparts spiritual gifts to Christian believers. This process is accomplished by the Spirit's choice or volition. He imparts gifts as He chooses (1 Corinthians 12:11).

The Spirit of God possesses all three of these characteristics. He is a He, not an it! This is a very important concept to have firmly imbedded in our understanding.

When we think about our relationship to the Spirit and what it means to walk in the Spirit or be filled with the Spirit, we are talking about how we are related to a person, not a force or substance. Much of the confusion surrounding the work and ministry of the Holy Spirit has its roots in the misunderstanding of this fact.

Fact Two—He Is God.

The second critical truth about the Holy Spirit that is essential to our understanding of how to plug into the power source of walking as God's men is the fact that the Holy Spirit is God. I don't know if there is any theological concept more complex than the truth that God is triune. The normal word chosen to articulate this fact is the word *Trinity*. God is one, but He is three. How does that work?

Historically, the men who have tried to define biblical faith have formulated this concept by saying that God is one in essence and three in person. The Bible is absolutely clear that there is only one God. In the great creedal statement of the people of Israel, Moses declared, "Hear, O Israel: The LORD our God, the LORD is one" (Deuteronomy 6:4). There is only one true God.

Most of us have little problem acknowledging that there is a God in Heaven whom we call the Father. As Christians we have come to believe that God came to earth in the flesh. We believe in Jesus Christ. Jesus was more than the Son of God. Jesus was God the Son. In Him, God was pleased to have all the fullness of the Deity dwell bodily (Colossians 1:19). The Apostle John tells us that in the beginning the Word was existing (John 1:1). He uses this Greek philosophical term—*Word*, or *Logos*, to describe the preincarnate Christ. He goes on to say that "the Word was with God, and the Word was God" (John1:1-2). The structure of these verses in the Greek text makes Jesus equal with the Father, yet distinct from the Father.

During His earthly ministry Jesus spent much time talking about and with the Father. Everything He did, He did in obedience to the Father's will while relying upon the Father's enabling. Yet, Jesus made statements like, "I and the Father are one" (John 10:30). The Father is God, and the Son is God, but there is only one God.

As if these concepts aren't baffling enough, along comes the Holy Spirit. Jesus told the disciples that the Holy Spirit was going to enter into a new relationship with them after Jesus returned to the Father. He had been *with* them, but now he was going to be *in* them. When the Spirit came to dwell in them, Jesus Himself would be in them, and the Father would also be in them (John 17:23). You see, wherever the Spirit is present Jesus is present, and wherever Jesus is present the Father is present. They are three, but they are one. If you tried to diagram this reality it might look something like this:

THE TRI-UNITY

The large circle represents the oneness of God. The three interpenetrating circles represent the three persons of the Trinity. The three persons are unique and distinct, but they also are one in essence. Their personalities interpenetrate. I know this is complex, but the point here is that in the same way Jesus is God and the Father is God, the Holy

Spirit is also God. This is a tremendous truth with immense implications in the quest to be God's man.

Think about it! When you received Jesus Christ as your Lord and Savior, and invited Him to come into your life, you were invaded by the Holy Spirit. You do not have some impersonal force dwelling in you. You were invaded by the third person of the Trinity. You have a person dwelling in you who is God. God is in you and available to help you live the Christian life. The Holy Spirit possesses all the attributes of the Deity. He is omniscient. You have the smartest person in the universe living in you. He is omnipotent. You have a person with infinite power living in you. He is all-wise, holy, just, loving, good, righteous, and perfect, and He has made His dwelling place in your inner being!

THE WORK OF THE SPIRIT

The work of the Holy Spirit is a wonderfully multifaceted subject. From the very beginning of our spiritual journey to the most sophisticated transformations that take place in our lives, the Holy Spirit is at work. He is the experiential link in the plan of God for our lives. You might say that everything the Father planned from eternity past, that was made possible by the work of the Son, is made real in our experience by the ministry of the Holy Spirit.

Before we ever committed our lives to Christ, the Holy Spirit was at work. All our lives we have lived out of conformity with the will of God. The Bible calls this reality sin. You and I were sinners from birth (Psalms 51:5). This fact has always been true of us, but we did not always know it. It is also true that all our lives the grace and forgiveness of Christ have been available to us, even though we have not been conscious of this fact, either.

One day, both of these truths began to become clear to us. We started to get in touch with the reality that something was fundamentally wrong with our lives. We had a sense that the way we were living and many of the things we were doing were wrong. What created this awareness? The Holy Spirit. Part of the work of the Spirit is to penetrate our denial systems and make us aware of our sin and our need for forgiveness. The process is called conviction.

Part of the process of conviction also involves helping us wake up to the reality of who Christ is and what He has done for us. I remember repeated instances where I heard about the death and resurrection of Jesus. This information meant nothing to me. I was a skeptic and an active critic of Christian things. Then one day I began to experience this process of conviction. I had no clue what was going on. All I knew was that now when friends talked to me about Christ, it began to make some sense. One night I was reading the third chapter of the Gospel of John. This was a minor miracle in and of itself! Somewhere in the midst of that reading it all came clear. Jesus was who He claimed to be! He was the Son of God who died for me and rose from the dead. He had power to come into my life and help me discover God's love and plan. I knew it with absolute certainty! This moment of clarity was the work of the Holy Spirit completing the work of conviction. I suddenly knew I was sunk and hopeless in myself and that Jesus was there to meet my need. This brought me to the most important moment of decision in my life. What happened next was again the work of the Holy Spirit.

I believe human beings are unable to respond to the grace of God apart from the grace of God enabling them to respond. Apart from the work of the Holy Spirit in enabling the moment of decision, I could not have received Jesus Christ. I knew I had a decision to make.

In some ways it was the most difficult decision of my life. I had been counting the cost of becoming a Christian for several months. Now the moment of truth had arrived and I didn't know if I could make the commitment. But something was happening in me. I was being enabled. I dropped to my knees by the side of my bed and prayed, *Lord Jesus, I know You are real. I need You. Thank You for dying on the cross for me. Come into my life and be my Lord and Savior.* I am absolutely convinced that the ability to sincerely pray that prayer was created in my inner being by the Holy Spirit. What happened next was truly miraculous.

As I prayed that prayer Jesus Christ came to dwell in my inner being. How did He do that? He sent the Spirit to dwell within me. Remember, wherever the Holy Spirit is present, Jesus is present. Jesus Christ took on a human body when He came to earth as the Savior. When He rose from the dead He still had a body. The disciples touched Him and even ate with Him. True, His body was significantly different from ours because it was a resurrection body like we will one day be given. But it was a flesh-and-bones body. When Jesus Christ ascended to the Father, He did so in a body. The Apostle Paul says that in Christ all the fullness of God dwells bodily (Colossians 2:9). The present tense verb of this statement in the Greek text confirms that Jesus still has a body. One day He will come again to finish what was started at the cross. On that day He will have a body. It will be a spiritual, eternal, incorruptible, glorious body, but it will be a body.

When we ask Jesus Christ to come into our lives, He does not come physically. He doesn't rip open our chest cavity and physically step into our hearts. That would be ridiculous. He comes into our lives by sending the Holy Spirit to indwell our spirit. The Holy Spirit becomes the agent through whom Christ comes. When that happens we come alive spiritually. The reality of spiritual regeneration and new birth are the work of the Holy Spirit. Spiritual death is the absence of the Spirit. He is the source of life. Jesus said, "The Spirit gives life" (John 6:63). Spiritual life is the presence of the Spirit. To be born of the Spirit is to be born again, anew, and from above (all meanings of the Greek word *anothen* used in John 3).

This all sounds too good to be true. To have God the Spirit invade our lives and give us new life is the greatest gift in the entire universe! But as great as it is, it is only the beginning of what the Holy Spirit wants to do in our lives. Instantly, when we receive the gift of Christ's love and forgiveness we are declared righteous in God's sight, not on the basis of our nonexistent righteousness, but on the basis of the righteousness of Jesus Christ being accounted to us. Remember, this is the meaning of being justified by faith. But God's plan for our lives is not just that we be accounted righteous in His eyes. He wants us to become righteous experientially. Guess how that happens? You guessed it: it is the work of the Holy Spirit.

The Holy Spirit is the *Holy* Spirit. Wherever He dwells He works to make that place holy also. In the Old Testament, the Spirit manifested the glory of God in the Tabernacle and Temple of Israel. Those were holy places because God was present by the Spirit. God never really wanted to dwell in a wood-and-stone building. The building He wants to inhabit is the one He created on the sixth day. He desires the human personality to be His temple and to manifest His glory through the lives of the men He has created. This was impossible when we were spiritually dead, because we didn't have the equipment. Now, in Christ, our lives have once again become the temple of God. How? By the presence of the Holy Spirit. Paul asked the believers in the ancient city of Corinth, "Don't you know that you yourselves are God's temple and that God's Spirit lives in you?" (1 Corinthians 3:16).

When the Holy Spirit takes up residence in our lives, He begins to work in us so that we can become a holy dwelling place. He begins a process of transformation called sanctification. The word *sanctify* means "to make holy." The Holy Spirit begins to change us from the inside out. His goal is to see us become conformed to the image of Jesus Christ (Romans 8:30). Becoming the men God always intended us to be is the work of the Holy Spirit. We have a part to play in this process also, but for now I want you to understand the important role the Holy Spirit plays.

As we grow in our relationship with Christ, we will begin to have a desire to do the things that would please God. We not only want to live in a way that is pleasing, we also find ourselves wanting to do things that serve God's Kingdom. This desire is a product of the Holy Spirit working in our motivational system. The work of the Kingdom of God is spiritual work. It requires equipment that we do not possess in our natural state. To accomplish this work every believer is endowed at the moment of regeneration with supernatural abilities called spiritual gifts (Romans 12:1-8). These gifts are bestowed by the Holy Spirit's presence and energized by the Spirit's enabling. When exercised in accordance with the will of God, the Holy Spirit empowers the use of the gift so that it bears spiritual fruit.

If you put all these facts about the Holy Spirit together, you can begin to see how critical our relationship with the Spirit is if we are going to be the men God intends us to be. In every dimension of authentic spiritual living the Holy Spirit is the agent of God's power who makes our walk possible. Our purpose in life is to be spiritual men. Only the Holy Spirit makes that possible.

SPIRIT-POWERED

Step three is a step of empowerment. We can tap into the empowering presence of the Holy Spirit in a way that will enable us to walk like godly men. Even though the Holy Spirit is present in every authentic, spiritually regenerate believer, He does not always have the kind of relationship with the believer that allows Him to do everything in and through the believer that He would like to. In order for that to occur we need to be filled with the Spirit (Ephesians 5:18).

There is a great deal of confusion and disagreement today within the Body of Christ about the specific way the power of the Holy Spirit is released in the life of the Christian. It seems a pity that something so wonderful should be such a source of division. It must be one of the great joys of the Enemy that the very dynamic enabling the believer to overcome him has become such an effective source of conflict. Let me attempt to simplify the process of empowerment.

Remember, the Holy Spirit is a person. Our relationship with the Spirit is expressed in the Bible by conceptual language, in the sense that words are used to attempt to describe or define spiritual realities. We might not be in total agreement about the language we use, but generally, we should all be desiring the same experience.

The beginning of empowerment comes with a realization of the indwelling of the Spirit. If you have invited Jesus Christ into your life as Lord and Savior, He has come. The only way He can come is by sending the Spirit to indwell you; therefore, if you have received Christ, you have the Holy Spirit in your life (Romans 8:9). Once the Spirit is present, it is God's will that the influence of the Spirit be the dominant factor in your inner life. This dominant influence is what the Bible calls being filled with the Spirit.

What does it mean to be filled with the Spirit? First of all, understand that this is to be the norm for the authentic believer. In the New Testament book of Ephesians the Apostle Paul writes, "Be filled with the Spirit" (Ephesians 5:18). In the Greek text the verb in this instruction is a present tense verb. This verb tense speaks of continual, ongoing action. In other words, the instruction might be understood as to "be being filled continually with the Spirit."

The word translated as "fill" in our English Bible is the Greek word *pleroo*. When used in this context it means "to be under the dominant influence of." Another way of saying the same thing would be "to be controlled, influenced, and empowered by." The most common mistake in understanding this concept is to think of the Holy Spirit as a substance instead of a person. When this conceptual error takes place, we begin to think of having more or less of the substance and tend to think of being filled as a process like filling a glass with water. When we remember that the Spirit is a person, we realize that this cannot be the case. What we need is not more of the Spirit as a substance. What we need is to experience more of the Holy Spirit as a person. Someone has accurately pointed out that the real issue is not us getting more of the Spirit but the Spirit getting more of us by our relinquishment to His influence.

To be filled with the Spirit requires an act of submission and appropriation. The act of submission involves a decision we must make about who we want to be the dominant influence in our life. Do we want the Spirit to be the ultimate controlling influence, or do we really want our own ego to control? One simple check in this area is to examine whether or not you desire to be empowered by the Spirit so that you can live obediently and accomplish God's will, or whether you simply have an egocentric desire for personal power to serve your own self. My own hunch is that many who have never had any encounter with the reality of the Spirit suffer from the illusion that the Holy Spirit releases His power for the second purpose. Nothing could be further from the truth.

If our lives and wills are surrendered to Christ, and our desire to be empowered is motivated by a longing to live obediently and be useful for God's purposes, then we are properly internally positioned to ask the Holy Spirit to fill our lives. This constitutes the heart of step three. God has promised in His Word that whenever we ask for something in prayer that is in conformity with His revealed will, we can have confidence that we will receive the thing we have asked for (1 John 5:14-15). We know that being filled with the Spirit is God's will because He has not only instructed us to be filled, He actually has commanded us to be filled. The verb *pleroo* is in the imperative mood in Ephesians 5:18. This means that being filled is not optional from God's standpoint. God's command assures us that if we ask, He will answer.

Jesus also taught the disciples that the Father delights in giving the Holy Spirit to those who ask for it in prayer (Luke 11:13). To take step three, use the gift of prayer and ask:

> Holy Spirit, fill my life with Your presence. Direct and empower my life. Work in and through me. Come upon me in power.

Can it really be that simple? Absolutely! It was costly to make it simple. It cost God the Cross to make it this easy. But for you and me, this simple step of relinquishment and appropriation makes the Spirit's presence active in an empowering way. If you have asked in sincerity, believe that your prayer has been answered. You might want to thank the Holy Spirit right now that He is filling your life. Thanking Him constitutes an act of faith, and faith makes the reality more experiential (Hebrews 11:1).

Now what? You not only want to be filled with the Spirit, you also want to "walk in the Spirit" (Galatians 5:25, KJV). Walking in the Spirit involves the process of keeping the Spirit's filling active, step by step, as we seek to be God's men. Every Spirit-filled step becomes part of the walk. In order to effectively walk in the Spirit we need to understand how to maintain Christ's lordship in our lives and what obstacles tend to get us off track. We'll look at those issues as we take step four.

CHECKPOINTS

Personal Reflection
1. Think about the Holy Spirit as a person.
2. How much of your will is surrendered to the Holy Spirit?
3. How would your life be different if you were walking in the Spirit?

Group Discussion
1. Share your first exposure to the concept of the Holy Spirit.
2. Tell about a time when you knew you were filled with the Spirit.
3. What is the greatest obstacle keeping you from walking in the Spirit?

4
STEP FOUR
MAINTAINING CHRIST'S LORDSHIP
In your hearts set apart Christ as Lord.
(1 Peter 3:15)

Lord Jesus, I willingly relinquish the throne
of my life and invite You to once again
take control as Lord of my life.

I saw him go over the edge. My insides immediately turned into a huge knot as I ran to the edge of the drop-off to see what shape my buddy was in. A group of men from our church were in the slums of Tijuana, Mexico, building a house for a family that was living in a big cardboard box. We were having a great time together and were almost finished with our part of the job.

The house we were building was on a steep hill. Houses had been built on top of other houses. Directly below the house we were building, another house had been cut into the side of the hill. Tom had failed to look where he was going as he stepped backward to admire our team's work. Without any warning he fell backward and headfirst into the excavation work of the house below ours. By the grace of God he didn't break his neck. Miraculously, he wasn't hurt at all! You have to be very cautious when you walk through the Tijuana dump. It is a hazardous place.

The spiritual walk is a lot like working in Tijuana. If

you are not careful, you will find yourself falling head over heels into dangerous territory. Some of the dangers of the walk are external. Others are internal. In this chapter I will attempt to help you understand some of the dangers and obstacles you will face as you seek to become God's man. Step four will be critical in keeping you on track with Christ, day by day, moment by moment.

SABOTAGED

When Jim climbed out of bed on Sunday morning, he thought he finally was going to get it right. After all, he had just returned from a wonderful men's conference where a string of nationally known speakers had convinced him of the need to make his wife and family a priority. He had recommitted his life to Christ and was ready to tackle his new resolutions. Then it all started falling apart.

It started to go wrong when his wife reminded him that since he had spent most of the weekend at the men's retreat, she really needed him to finish cleaning the garage as soon as he got home from church. She had been bugging him about this job for several months, and the mere mention of the garage gave him a sensation like a set of fingernails scraping across a blackboard. Suddenly, all the warm and loving feelings he had conjured toward his wife at the retreat started to fade.

No sooner had Mary finished her appeal than the door flew open and the kids came screaming into the room arguing about who got to have the strawberry instant oatmeal and who had to eat the cinnamon and spice. Maintaining control for a few more minutes, Jim managed to get a shower and get dressed to take the family to church. Too bad the car wouldn't start! While the kids shouted at each other in the back seat, Mary reminded him that she had told him he should have taken the car in for its annual checkup. Somewhere in the middle of this scene Jim felt something snap. Before he knew what had happened he had yelled at the kids, told his wife that maybe once in her life she could do something about maintaining the car herself, stepped out of the car, and slammed the door, leaving his family in stunned silence.

When the dust settled, Jim felt defeated. He wondered what had gone wrong. With minor variations this kind of experience happens all the time to men who are actually trying to be God's men and get it right. Suddenly, all our good intentions have been sabotaged and we find ourselves in a state of mind that we know does not please God. Although our initial reaction is usually one of discouragement about the whole Christian adventure, we should realize that this internal conflict is very normal and should be expected in our walk. Jim's little blowup reflects the first major obstacle most of us encounter in learning to be a true Christian man. We have discovered the first enemy, and it is us!

FLESH PREVENTION

Over the years of "fighting the good fight" I have developed an approach to winning this internal struggle that I call flesh prevention. This approach involves several steps that I hope will help you win the battle. The first step has to do with understanding the dynamics of the conflict. There are certain dynamics of your internal landscape that are critically important to understand, and there are certain realities of the world in which we live which also need to be recognized if we are going to effectively win the battle.

The Inner Dynamics

I often have the privilege of speaking to men about the problem Jim experienced on his return from the conference. I usually begin by saying something like, "I've got some good news about the Christian life, and I've got some bad news. The good news is that once you have opened your life to Jesus Christ and received Him as Savior and Lord, Christ is in you. The bad news is that you are still in you!" The internal landscape of the man of God always contains these two realities.

Christ in you, by the indwelling presence of the Holy Spirit, is good news. Once you have experienced spiritual rebirth, you possess what the Bible calls a new nature. You have become a new creature in Christ (2 Corinthians 5:17). At the same time you still have within you all the same propensities to live a life totally dominated by your own fallen ego. This part of your inner life is referred to in the New Testament by the term *flesh*. Synonyms include *old nature, sinful nature,* and others.

At the core of your being a battle is being waged between these two realities. The Apostle Paul talks about this conflict in the book of Galatians where he states, "The sinful nature [flesh] desires what is contrary to the Spirit, and the Spirit what is contrary to the sinful nature [flesh]. They are in conflict with each other" (Galatians 5:17).

Believe it or not, even Paul, as well as all the other apostles and great men of God throughout the centuries, waged this battle. So take heart, you are in good company! The problem for many men is that they never understand the conflict or how to win the battle.

To help myself remember these two realities I developed the following diagram:

INTERNAL DRIVE STRUCTURE

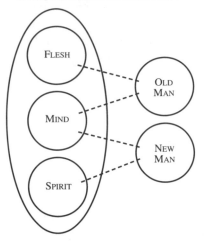

The three circles on the left represent the three primary drive structures that are at work in the inner life of the man who has come to know Christ. The top circle represents that part of your inner being that is called the flesh or the old nature. What do we mean when we use the word *nature*? One of my seminary professors attempted to describe a nature as a propensity or inclination. This is an internal condition that is a product of our physiology, psychology, and spirituality before we became Christ's men.

Notice that when the mind is operating in conjunction with this inner drive factor the product is what the Bible calls the *old man*. The Bible tells us that the spiritual condition of the old man is death. By that it means that we are cut off from the life of God and fellowship with God when the flesh controls and dominates our life.

The mind is the control center of our life. By using the mind we choose how we are going to live. All behavior begins in this part of our inner life. If you take a piece of paper and cover the bottom two circles on the diagram, you have a schematic of your life before you received Jesus Christ. The mind set on the flesh was your only option. What was the result? You lived in the flesh.

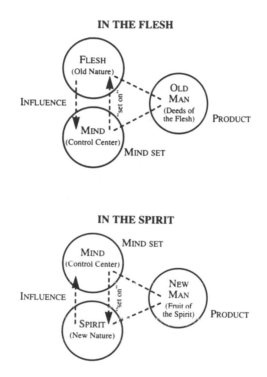

IN THE FLESH

IN THE SPIRIT

Since this part of our inner being was developed apart from God's influence, it is extremely distorted. In describing the conflict of the old and the new in the letter to the churches of Galatia, Paul gives a vivid description of what the flesh generates in our lives:

The acts of the sinful nature [flesh] are obvious: sexual immorality, impurity and debauchery; idolatry and witchcraft; hatred, discord, jealousy, fits of rage, selfish ambition, dissensions, factions and envy; drunkenness, orgies, and the like. (Galatians 5:19-21)

It's not a pretty picture, is it? No wonder Paul says, "I know that nothing good lives in me, that is, in my sinful nature [flesh]" (Romans 7:18). If we are brutally honest with ourselves, isn't this what much of our life looked like apart from Christ? Our intellect had been programmed with faulty thought patterns. Our emotions were constantly responding to our wounded and warped egos. Our lives were filled with bad habit patterns produced by a self-centered will. These same tendencies are still at work in our life even after we have come to know Christ. The challenge is learning how to overcome these propensities and inclinations and walk in the Spirit rather than in the flesh.

The secret to overcoming the top circle is to learn to identify when the influences exerting pressure on our lives are coming from this internal drive structure. Then having identified the pull of the flesh, we need to understand the alternative. The real key to overcoming the top circle is to operate out of the bottom circle of the Spirit. Because the Holy Spirit has come to indwell our lives, we now have the possibility of making a choice. Remove the paper covering the bottom two circles. Notice that the mind is positioned between the flesh and the Spirit. The mind now has the ability to say no to the flesh and choose to respond to the Spirit. This is what Paul means by the mind set on the flesh and the mind set on the Spirit (Romans 8:5).

When we choose to allow the Holy Spirit to be the dominant influence in our lives, we experience the reality the Bible calls the new man. If you want to know whether or not this is the dominant influence in your life, go back to Galatians 5 where Paul identified the products of the old nature. Following the bleak portrait painted in verses 19-22, Paul now describes what the indwelling of Christ by the ministry of the Holy Spirit can produce in our life: "The fruit of the Spirit is love, joy, peace, patience, kindness, goodness, faithfulness, gentleness and self-control" (Galatians 5:22-23).

What a contrast! First look at the "acts of the sinful nature" and then look at the "fruit of the Spirit." These are the options our internal dynamics are constantly capable of. Which would you like to characterize your life? Why then is this such a tough battle? The reason is that these two natures create an internal conflict that is difficult. Go back a few verses in Galatians 5 and look again at how Paul describes it:

> So I say, live by the Spirit, and you will not gratify the desires of the sinful nature [flesh]. For the sinful nature [flesh] desires what is contrary to the Spirit, and the Spirit what is contrary to the sinful nature [flesh]. They are in conflict with each other, so that you do not do what you want. (Galatians 5:16-17)

I again have some good news and some bad news. The good news is that conflict is normative. The bad news is that conflict is normative. In my own experience and ministry this has proven itself true. Let's go back to where we started this chapter and look at these forces at work.

SABOTAGE REVISITED

Let's put Jim and Mary's blowup in reverse and rewind to the beginning of the conflict. Then, let's take a look at Jim's internal drive structures. What do we see? Jim is off to a good start. He has spent the early part of the weekend at the men's conference. He has recommitted his life to Christ. He has invited Jesus Christ to live and reign in his life. His mind has been set on the Spirit. As a result, with the Spirit in control, Jim has decided to work at being a better husband and father. These are good and proper resolutions that have been generated as a product of his positive spiritual encounter.

Now Jim is down off the "mountaintop" and back into the valley of daily life. Mary is a bit bugged. She has had a hard weekend with the kids while Jim was away. Mary is a Christian, too. Like Jim, she doesn't understand the dynamics of her inner life. If she did, at the beginning of her irritation she might have sensed that the flesh was beginning to influence her thinking, and she could have made a choice about what to do with her anger. As it is, what could have been a reasonable request, made with the right attitude, and in the right tone of voice, has become a grumbling complaint that is coming right out of the mind set on the flesh.

Most marital conflict between believing husbands and wives is a direct product of ego clashes. When Mary deals with Jim in the flesh, the flesh in Jim stands up and takes notice. Right at this point, Jim, if he had been conscious of what was happening internally, had a choice of his own to make. If he responded to Mary's irritability with irritability of his own, he would know that he was beginning to set his mind on the flesh. If, on the other hand, he had recognized his internal response as one of irritability and identified that something was wrong with this response, he could have made a different choice. Which internal dynamic produces irritability? The fruit of the Spirit is patience. How could Jim have responded to Mary with patience? He could have said no to the flesh and immediately asked Christ to take control of his response. Then he could have set his mind on the Spirit by choosing to be patient as God enabled him. All this can happen in a split second with hardly a conscious thought when we learn to identify our internal dynamics and understand that the Spirit makes an alternative possible. Over time, and with maturity, the positive response of the Spirit can become as much a habit as the negative response of the flesh.

Instead, what do we see? Jim doesn't understand what is happening. He feels internally conflicted, because he *is* internally conflicted. This is normal, but Jim begins to think that something must be wrong. His own irritability begins to grow. Circumstances continue to get worse. They always do, by the way! The kids begin to irritate him. The car won't start. Mary puts the finishing touches on the situation with one good "I told you so." Jim goes ballistic. He is in the flesh and he is feeling defeated.

It didn't need to happen. If we are going to live more effectively when faced with angry spouses and broken-down cars, we need to know these dynamics. As if this isn't challenging enough, at the same time these conflicts are working internally there is another set of external forces at work in the unseen dimension of what I call the real world.

THE REAL WORLD

I love winter mornings in Colorado. Rolling out of bed, I can see the freshly fallen snow on the ground as I head downstairs for my early morning time of prayer. Stopping in the kitchen, I start the coffee brewing before I head for the living room and my special "prayer chair." With a cup of hot coffee in hand I settle down and look out the window of our living room at the front range of the snow-covered Rockies. From this vantage point the world is beautiful.

On this particular morning I am drinking coffee from one of my favorite mugs. The outside of the cup is covered with pictures of wild animals, dressed in business suits, heading toward a metropolitan skyline. On the inside rim of the cup, positioned so that I see it as I drink, is the message "IT'S A JUNGLE OUT THERE!" This cup always reminds me of why I have rolled out of bed an hour early to pray. It is a jungle out there! As a matter of fact, it is a war zone.

The virgin snow covering the pristine landscape touches some deep chord of longing within for that which no longer exists in this world. The beauty and purity of the morning will soon fade as I leave the warmth of my home and head out into a fallen world filled with both seen and unseen dangers. My worldview helps me understand the real world and motivates me to become spiritually prepared to live effectively for the Kingdom of Christ in the midst of a fallen world.

My philosophy professor in college was a German atheist. He used to challenge us to understand our *weltanschauung*. The word means "worldview." At the time I was quite sure I didn't have one. After I became a Christian I started to understand how critically important this internal picture of the world is. Our worldview will to a great extent shape how we live. Several years ago I created a simple tool to remind me of the essential components of the external factors influencing my daily walk. I call it the Real-World Matrix.

REAL WORLD MATRIX

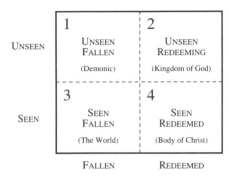

The matrix is composed of four quadrants, which represent components or parts of a holistic understanding of the universe in which we live. I use the phrase "the real world" because of the belief in our culture that only that which is seen is real. Nothing could be further from the truth! Any worldview that fails to incorporate the unseen realities of the spiritual universe is actually an unreal worldview. Thus, the four quadrants of the matrix are derived by recognizing that part of the real world is seen — that is, the physical reality of the created universe — while part of the real world is unseen. The top two quadrants belong to the unseen reality of the spiritual universe. The bottom quadrants belong to the seen physical universe. The left quadrants are separated from the right by the spiritual reality of the dichotomy which exists between that which is fallen and that which is redeemed.

Quadrant 1 represents the reality of the unseen fallen universe. The existence of this quadrant reminds us that the world of the demonic is very real. We need to be reminded of this reality on a daily basis. Quadrant 2 represents all the heavenly realities of the Kingdom of God. This quadrant is the source of redemption. All authentic, biblical spiritu-ality will flow from this sector of the matrix. Quadrant 3 represents the visible fallen world of human culture and society. Quadrant 4 contains all tangible expressions of the Kingdom, which have invaded the world through the work of Christ and the ministry of the Spirit.

These four quadrants combine to make up the real world. As I work at being God's man, I must recognize that every day all four are part of the world in which I live. I have certain relationships with each quadrant which constitute critical dynamics of my daily walk. For instance, before I became a Christian, my life was centered in Quadrant 3. I was *in* and *of* the world. The unredeemed world system is constantly influenced by the fallen demonic forces represented by Quadrant 1. The Apostle Paul reminds the Ephesian Christians that formerly they had "followed the ways of this world and of the ruler of the kingdom of the air, the spirit who is now at work in those who are disobedient" (Ephesians 2:2).

BEFORE CHRIST

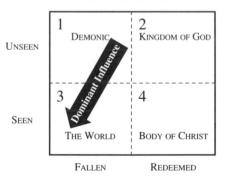

Fortunately, or I should say graciously, somewhere along the line I began to be influenced by the realities of the Kingdom of God represented by Quadrant 2. The Holy Spirit began to work in my life as friends who had already become Christians prayed for me, ministered to me, and began witnessing to me. As a result, one day I dropped to my knees and invited Jesus Christ to come into my life. Instantly, the center of my life shifted from Quadrant 3 into Quadrant 4. Paul speaks of this shift in Colossians when he says that in Christ, God has "rescued us from the dominion of darkness and brought us into the kingdom of the Son he loves" (Colossians 1:13).

With this transaction complete, the predominant influences in my life could now come from the heavenly realities of Quadrant 2. I learned to pray and read the Word. These two disciplines enabled me to access Kingdom realities and appropriate the empowerment of the Spirit to live effectively out of Quadrant 4.

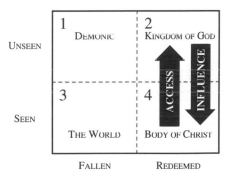

IN CHRIST

SPIRITUAL WARFARE

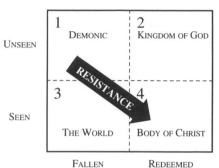

TEMPTATION

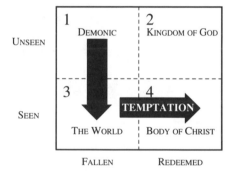

During this period of time my worldview began to go through radical transformation. I began to experience a new kind of difficulty coming from the unseen demonic realm. Paul refers to this difficulty a little later in his letter to the Ephesians when he reminds them that "our struggle is not against flesh and blood, but against the rulers, against the authorities, . . . against the spiritual forces of evil in the heavenly realms" (Ephesians 6:12). This was the beginning of my understanding of the reality of spiritual warfare. Along with the internal conflict of the flesh and the Spirit, I was involved in an unseen external conflict with the forces of spiritual darkness.

I also began to look at the fallen world quite differently. At times I experienced an inexplicable longing to return to some of the activities which characterized my life in the old quadrant. My new understanding of the real world helped me resist this temptation as I realized that much of the seductive power of Quadrant 3 actually is a product of Quadrant 1 activity.

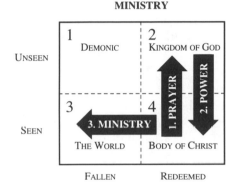

When not being lured by the world system, I began to experience a desire to invade it for the sake of Christ. This desire came from the influence God was building in my life to be a ministry force for His Kingdom in the world. Often these desires and attempts to express them met with wonderful success. Success usually seemed to have a correlation with how much time I spent drawing upon the resources of Quadrant 2, praying on behalf of friends who still didn't understand who Christ is and how He loves them.

Sometimes my efforts seemed to meet with great resistance. This reminded me of how strong a grasp the Evil One has on the world. At these times the only truth that kept me from becoming discouraged was the recognition that the real battle was being waged in the heavenly realm and the ultimate outcome of that conflict was already assured (Colossians 2:15).

LIVING IN THE REAL WORLD

Recognizing the reality of the four components of the real world has shaped my worldview. I finally have a weltanschauung. Every day all the dynamics of all four quadrants are constantly influencing our lives. This is the real world and we need to know how to effectively interact with it and live in a way that maximizes the influence of the Kingdom of God and minimizes the influence of the fallen, demonic realities of life. Let's go back again and see how the external dynamics of the real world, interacting with the internal dynamics of Jim and Mary's internal drive structures, led to Jim's self-defeating blowup.

Over the weekend, Jim was firmly established in Quadrant 4. The retreat had been a great time of exposing him to much Quadrant 2 empowerment. Divine intervention had been taking place and Kingdom transformation was the result. At the same time all these great spiritual things were happening in Jim's life, it was as if an air-raid siren went off in Quadrant 1. The Evil One was losing ground in Jim's life and needed to launch a counter-attack to attempt to gain it back. Knowing Jim as he does, Satan perceives that the Achilles heel in Jim's spiritual experience is his temper. He also knows that the weekend has been difficult for Mary. He has seen to that! The stage is set. War is waged. Quadrant 1 influence is coming fast and furious at Quadrant 4.

Once Jim and Mary allowed their inner dynamics to move into flesh territory, they became prime candidates for becoming spiritual casualties. As Christians, the war is already won, but the battles are still being fought. If Satan can effectively capitalize on the flesh and create a blowup, Jim will get discouraged and Mary will become disillusioned. Maybe he can even plant that thought again in her mind that "It will never work out. I think we need to get a divorce. Jim is never going to change."

The picture is even more complex than this. You see, Jim and Mary are about to run into Don and Jan. Don and Jan are long-time friends of Jim and Mary's who are not Christians. Jim and Mary have been praying for them. Don and Jan live in Quadrant 3. As Jim and Mary have prayed, Quadrant 2 influence has been at work in Don and Jan's life. They are beginning to have interest in spiritual things. Today will be a very critical encounter. What will Don and Jan see when they run into Jim and Mary? Will they see a husband and wife who are being loving to one another and reflecting the love Christ has for the Church? I think not. They will see a husband and wife in serious conflict with the flesh in control. This encounter will be a setback for Jim and Mary penetrating Quadrant 3 with Quadrant 4 ministry effectiveness.

THRONE CHECK

How do you put all this together and live in a way that enables you to be God's man and maintain Christ's lordship in your life? If you take all the data contained in this chapter and pull it together, I believe you can create a simple tool to help keep yourself on track and to help get you back on track if you blow it. I call it a throne check.

Early in my own walk with Christ I was taught to think of a conceptual place in my inner life that was like a throne. This "throne" was the place of ultimate control over my life. At any given moment the throne would be occupied by either Jesus Christ or my ego or self-will. Before I asked Christ into my life, self or ego always occupied the throne. I was what the Apostle Paul called the natural man or man without the Spirit (1 Corinthians 2:14). The word used in this text is the word *psuchikos*. It is built on the word *psuche*, which in the Greek language was a word for natural, physical life, devoid of the Spirit. With ego on the throne, I lived in the flesh. It was my only option.

BEFORE CHRIST

When I asked Jesus Christ to come into my life, I made a decision to relinquish the throne of my life. I dethroned ego and enthroned Christ as Lord. This decision is the essence of what the Bible calls repentance. Only one person can occupy the throne. Until self is dethroned, Jesus cannot be Lord of my life. With Christ on the throne, I became what Paul calls a spiritual man (1 Corinthians 2:15).

CHRIST ENTHRONED

In this verse Paul uses the word *pnuematikos*. This word is built on the word *pnuema*, which is the Greek word for spirit. The spiritual man has Christ on the throne and lives under the dominant influence of the Holy Spirit. This is the goal of learning to live the Christian life. We want to consistently have this picture represent what is happening in our inner life.

CHRIST DETHRONED

Unfortunately, there is a third possibility. Because we are free, Christ never reigns without our permission. As a result, we can make choices and take actions which have the effect of dethroning Christ and once again enthroning our own ego. This reality is what Paul calls the fleshly man or worldly man (1 Corinthians 3:1). The word used here is *sarkinos*. It comes from the Greek word *sarx*, which we translate "flesh." Notice that Christ is still in the life, but self is in control. The result is that the man in this state is once again living in the flesh.

How do you know who is on the throne? You make a throne check. You stop and simply think about who is in control in any given moment. If you are conscious that self has taken over by blatant disobedience or sin, you know who is on the throne. Or maybe through spiritual negligence self has slowly crept up and taken over. In either case, Paul's list from Galatians 5 can serve as an inventory. What is the fruit of your life? Is it the deeds of the flesh or the fruit of the Spirit?

TAKING STEP FOUR

How do you get Christ back on the throne? It is amazingly simple. First, you have to want Him there. He is the consummate gentleman of the universe. He only responds to our desire and invitation. Once we are conscious that ego is on the throne, and assuming we want Christ there, we simply need to decide to dethrone ego again by an act of the will and invite Jesus to take control of the throne. We then ask Him to once again fill our lives with the presence and power of the Holy Spirit.

This spiritual exercise needs to be cultivated as a conscious habit in our lives. At first we might find ourselves working through this process a great many times during the day. As we grow and mature in our relationship with Christ we will naturally (or should I say supernaturally?) learn to maintain His lordship for longer periods with greater consistency. Maintaining His lordship is the task of step four. To take step four, pray something like this:

Lord Jesus, I willingly relinquish the throne of my life and invite You to once again take control as Lord of my life.

Once you sincerely pray that prayer, you have taken step four. You are positioned to move forward as God's man. You don't need to be spiritually paralyzed by remaining in a spiritual condition that is characterized by guilt and condemnation. In essence, retaking the throne of our lives is sin. As such it is often accompanied by actions that create a break in our fellowship with God and create what you might think of as spiritual soul pollution. To effectively live the Christian life requires that when we sin we know how to appropriate the cleansing power of Christ's forgiveness. Step five teaches us how to tap into the full effects of the Atonement on a daily basis. If you're ready, let's take the next step.

CHECKPOINTS

Personal Reflection
1. When was the last time you were sabotaged as Jim was?
2. Read and reflect on the conflict between your new nature (as in 2 Corinthians 5:17) and the flesh (as in Galatians 5:17).
3. Read and reflect on the deeds of the flesh in Galatians 5:19-21.
4. What Quadrant 1 activity is hindering your walk with Christ?
5. Think about your own worldview. Is it realistic? What factors may have helped shape your worldview? Do you take seriously the unseen realities of the spiritual world?

Group Discussion
1. Share with each other a time you were sabotaged.
2. Discuss together the Real-World Matrix.
3. What deed of the flesh gives you the greatest difficulty?

5

STEP FIVE
EXPERIENCING SPIRITUAL CLEANSING

If we confess our sins, he is faithful and just
and will forgive us our sins and purify us
from all unrighteousness.
(1 John 1:9)

Lord Jesus, I am a sinner constantly in need of Your
grace and the experience of Your forgiveness. Help me
be honest with You today. I will confess, repent,
and make restitution where appropriate.

November 7, 1949, was a monumental day in my personal history. On that illustrious date I made my first
appearance on planet earth. This fact tells you certain vital
information about who I am. First, you can easily calculate
my age. Second, you will notice that I am a part of that
unique fraternity of human beings called baby boomers.
Third, if you were born anywhere near that date you will
instantly realize that I was in high school and college during
the period of American history known as the sixties.

In many ways I am a product of the sixties. I loved the
Beatles, the Rolling Stones, long hair, tie-dyed T-shirts,
Woodstock, and just about every other signature characteristic of the period. I guess you could say I was a
bonafide pseudohippie. Almost every aging baby boomer
I know would like you to think he was a hippie in the
sixties, but those of us who were there know there was one
tell-tale trait that separated the hard-core hippies from the
mass of psuedohippies. Hard-core hippies didn't like to
take baths. This was why I could never have been one.

I like being clean. I love stepping out of the shower and feeling fresh and clean all over. This is probably a product of my days as an athlete. The best part of any workout or practice was always the time when the coach finally blew the whistle and uttered those words we had all been longing to hear: "Hit the showers!" Something about that magic moment has remained with me through the years. As great as it feels to experience the refreshing experience of physical cleansing, it can't compare with the wonderful experience of spiritual cleansing. Understanding how to experience spiritual cleansing is a critical step in learning how to become a Christian man.

Do you remember how it was when you first learned to walk? Probably not. If you have had the joy of raising children of your own, you definitely remember every step of their early days as a toddler. At first it looked something like this: take a step . . . fall down . . . get up . . . take a step . . . fall down . . . get up. After a while it began to get better: take a step . . . take another step . . . take a third step . . . fall down . . . take a step . . . take a step . . . take a step . . . fall down. Eventually, our children learned to walk without falling down. Periodically, they took a tumble and needed a hand, but there was a measure of progress that came with growth.

What was true in our physical development is also true in our spiritual development. Very few of us learn how to walk without taking a few spills. When we "fall down" spiritually we get dirty. We need to know how to get back up and get cleaned off.

WE ARE ALL BOZOS ON THIS BUS

I love being a Christian. I call it the ultimate no-lose proposition.

Think about it! In every other arena of our lives we are evaluated on the basis of our performance. If you were ever an athlete, your performance dictated your opportunity to participate. You moved through various levels of competition until your performance peaked. After your performance peaked, you lost the opportunity to move on to the next level. For most of us that was a very difficult moment. At forty-three I've finally come to grips with the fact that I am never going to be a running back in the NFL.

The same was true of our education. As long as we performed successfully we could move on to the next level of academic achievement. For many of us, our performance dictated which career we were able to pursue. Failure led to limitation.

Then came career. Talk about performance! Many men live day in, day out under the pressure of performing at work. They know that when performance begins to slip, the job is in jeopardy.

There is only one problem with the performance syndrome: we all fail eventually. That is why I love being a Christian. It is the one reality of my life that is not based on my performance.

I became a Christian on the basis of my failure and Jesus Christ's performance. The Body of Christ is the one organization in the world where the only requirement for membership is failure. The Church is a corporate gathering of a bunch of failures. Our motto is Romans 3:23: "For all have sinned [past-completed action] and fall short [present-ongoing action in the Greek] of the glory of God." I like to paraphrase this verse by saying, " We're all bozos on this bus!"

Jon is a new Christian. He grew up in a highly religious and rigidly strict family where God was viewed as the ultimate cosmic policeman. Guilt was a way of life in his family and his church. Somehow, Jon never figured out where Jesus Christ fit into all this. As soon as Jon left home for college he quit going to church. By the time he graduated from college he wasn't even sure he believed in God. During his days in law school he became an expert in every area of behavior that his childhood experience taught as taboo.

After ten years in practice Jon had become one of the most prominent and successful corporate attorneys in his city. He had a reputation as a cutthroat negotiator.

Two divorces hardly fazed him, but the day his son walked out of the house and told him he was the biggest jerk in the world, Jon finally began to crumble.

During this period of time Jon had a few friends who kept inviting him to a men's Bible study group. Jon not only resisted, he often responded to their invitations with blatant hostility. By the grace of God his buddies never gave up. One Tuesday morning Jon wandered into the fellowship hall of the church where several hundred men from the business community were gathered for an hour of fellowship and teaching. That morning the study was on the gift of God's grace as it is articulated in the third chapter of Romans. Something happened that morning. God touched Jon's life and Jon gave his heart to Jesus Christ, receiving Him as Savior and Lord.

Like many men, Jon did not find following Christ an easy task. He continued to wrestle with many old habit patterns from his old way of life. Jon had liked to drink hard and chase women. When not in court his vocabulary would have made a sailor blush. He had an angry streak rooted in childhood abuse that flared whenever the inner "wound" was touched.

The temptations Jon faced were great, and he didn't

always win the struggle. When he failed, he felt guilty and dirty inside. As a result, too often, Jon was defeated and felt like giving up the Christian life. What he really needed was to learn how to experience God's grace, forgiveness, and spiritual cleansing. Jon needed to learn how to get back up and live the Christian life.

THE REALITY OF SIN

Jon is not alone in this battle. He is simply a more blatant example of the struggle we all face with an enemy called sin. We all need the ongoing experience of forgiveness and cleansing. To understand why this is the case, it might be helpful to understand more about the reality of this problem the Bible calls sin.

Sin is any violation of God's moral imperative in attitude, action, or intent. Three Greek words are used in the New Testament to communicate this concept. *Hamartia* is the most generic word for sin. This is the word used in Romans 3:23 where Paul teaches that all have sinned. The word literally means "to miss the mark." The mark is the character and nature of God Himself. Any action, attitude, or intention that is not in conformity with the perfect holiness of God is sin. It misses the mark. Maybe you can begin to see why sin is such a universal problem.

A second word used to communicate the concept of sin is the Greek word *paraptoma*. This word is often translated "trespass." The word carries with it the sense of a false step which violates a boundary. What distinguishes a trespass from the third sin word, *parabasis*, is that a trespass is unintentional while a *parabasis*, or transgression, tends to be willful. The result of any of these three types of failure is the creation of true moral guilt. True moral guilt is the product of a life in which we have done what we ought not to have done and failed to do what we should have done.

True moral guilt is not the same as guilt feelings. You can have guilt feelings over something as innocent as eating too much Haagen-Dazs ice cream. True moral guilt is what I call a real reality. It is an internal, external, and cosmic reality that must be resolved.

FUTILE SOLUTIONS

How do you get rid of true moral guilt? Before we answer that question, let's take a look at how some men ineffectively attempt to deal with the problem. There are three primary futile solutions which most men use to deal with the problem of true moral guilt.

Denial
Brad is what many men would call a man's man. He is a foreman for one of the largest commercial construction companies in his area. He works hard, and for many years he has played hard. His lifestyle has not been without cost, however. Like many of the men Brad works with, he is divorced. He rarely gets to see his children because he was abusive as a father and the court has restricted his visiting privileges. Since the divorce, and actually long before it, Brad has lived a fast life. He drinks hard, drives fast, and likes to chase women. Brad has created a huge personal reservoir of true moral guilt.

To the casual observer Brad's experience would seem to contradict the belief that guilt takes its toll. His lifestyle doesn't seem to bother him at all. He actually appears to take a certain pride in the way he lives. If you confronted him about his lifestyle, he would deny that he is doing anything wrong. What happens to his guilt? It gets denied and internalized. This is a tactic that has been employed by men since the beginning of time. But what we see on the outside doesn't always reveal what is happening on the inside.

Things actually aren't going all that well for Brad. Late at night when he is home alone and the carousing is over, he feels a growing sense of despair. Brad is getting fatigued more easily and his strength feels sapped. He went to see his doctor because of increasing stomach problems only to discover that he has an ulcer. When Brad looks in the mirror in the morning, he doesn't like what he sees. To deny and internalize guilt is a strategy technically called repression. Most of us have employed it at one time or another. It doesn't work.

Reeducation
A second futile approach to the problem of guilt is one I call reeducation. There is a great deal of reeducation taking place in the world today. The thinking behind this approach goes something like this: If you do something that makes you feel guilty, it is probably because you have been taught that what you are doing is wrong. Therefore, if you don't want to feel guilty, decide that what you were taught to be wrong is actually right. Call black white and white black.

This approach raises the issue of a man's standard of authority. If what we were taught concerning right and wrong was rooted in the revelation of God in the Bible, and then we use the standard of relative cultural humanism to redefine right and wrong, we will have a serious problem. Not only will we fail to deal with the problem of true moral guilt, we will actually be facilitating the creation of massive new guilt.

Brad grew up in a Christian home. His parents taught

him that immorality was wrong. Early in his marriage Brad had the opportunity to cheat on his wife. He made a bad choice. Rather than getting honest with himself and God, he began to justify his actions and drifted from his early beliefs. After the divorce Brad began engaging in multiple sexual encounters. Over time he convinced himself there was nothing wrong with sex outside of marriage. He learned to practice the fine art of reeducation. But there is a problem: he is dying inside. His mind and his heart are out of sync. It isn't working. No amount of reeducation can change the moral fabric of the universe and the absolute nature of right and wrong. Reeducation doesn't work.

Self-Atonement

The final ineffective solution to the guilt problem is to be found in the various forms of self-atonement. From the guilt-motivated humanitarianism of the corporate mogul to the empty religiosity of the real-life Church Ladies of the world, self-atonement does not remove true moral guilt. Even many forms of self-punishment, ranging from certain forms of depression to various addictive behaviors, are at times unconscious attempts to atone for guilt by punishing oneself.

All of these approaches share two common characteristics. One: they don't work. And two: ultimately, they will destroy you. Sin and guilt are destructive. They require resolution.

THE GIFT OF FORGIVENESS

How do you resolve true moral guilt? It requires forgiveness. It requires forgiveness from the one person we always offend when we miss the mark, stumble over the boundaries, or willfully violate the moral imperative.

True moral guilt can only be forgiven by God, and even God had to pay a price to make forgiveness possible.

The central theme of the Bible, both Old and New Testaments, is the theme of forgiveness. God longs to forgive His children and cleanse them of the defilement sin creates in their lives. From the sacrificial system of the Law to the message given through the prophets, the Old Testament is filled with promises of a coming means of forgiveness and spiritual cleansing. This promise found its fulfillment in Jesus Christ.

The only adequate basis for solving the problem of true moral guilt is the forgiveness provided by God as a gift. This forgiveness is always rooted in the atoning work of Jesus Christ, accomplished on our behalf as He hung on a cross outside the city of Jerusalem nearly two thousand years ago. The message of the New Testament gospel is simple: "Christ died for our sins" (1 Corinthians 15:3). How did the death of Jesus solve the problem of guilt? Let me paint a word picture for you drawn from Paul's letter to the Colossians.

In the second chapter of Colossians, Paul makes the following declaration:

> When you were dead in your sins and in the uncircumcision of your sinful nature, God made you alive with Christ. He forgave us all our sins, having canceled the written code, with its regulations, that was against us and that stood opposed to us; he took it away, nailing it to the cross. (Colossians 2:13-14)

This passage is rich in both cultural and spiritual significance. Under Roman law, when a man violated the law and was found guilty by a court of law, a written charge was drawn up detailing the individual's offense or offenses. Often, the jails of the ancient world were located in close proximity to the public marketplace. The written charge against the guilty party was placed on the outside of the cell so that anyone passing by could look at the prisoner and immediately know the offense for which he was serving time. As you can imagine, this was quite an effective deterrent to crime!

In capital cases during the time of Christ, crucifixion was the means by which the death sentence was executed. In the case of crucifixion, the written charge, or *epigraphon*, was attached to the cross of the criminal. Crucifixion also took place along public thoroughfares so that all citizens could see the terrible price of committing a capital offense. In all four gospel accounts of the trial and crucifixion of Jesus we are told that Pilate had a written charge prepared and fastened to the cross. It read, "The King of the Jews" (Matthew 27:37, Mark 15:26, Luke 23:38, John 19:19). Both Mark and Luke use the word *epigraphon* to describe this document. John further informs us that it was written in three languages so that all passing by could clearly understand why Jesus was being crucified.

The religious leaders were incensed by Pilate's actions. They wanted the charge to read that Jesus *claimed* to be king of the Jews, thus indicating treason or blasphemy. Pilate refused. In essence, Pilate was affirming that Jesus was being innocently put to death. Hold that image for a moment while I weave for you another strand of the tapestry.

In Colossians Paul speaks of the written charge or code that was against us. Paul uses the Greek word *cheirographon* in this text. This word is very similar to *epigraphon*, but was more of a business term than a judicial one. It is sometimes translated as "certificate of debt." In the business world of Paul's day, if you owed a person money, a legal instrument called a *cheirographon* was created to specify the terms of the debt. It listed what was owed and what needed to be done to repay the debt.

Paul uses this concept to illustrate the result of our sin. Each of us has created a spiritual certificate of debt owed to God. You might imagine this as a document listing every action, attitude, and intention of your heart that violate the moral imperative of God. This would be a comprehensive document including all sins, trespasses, and transgressions past, present, and future. As such, this spiritual document would itemize every source of true moral guilt in each of our lives. For most of us it would not be a pretty piece of paper!

In the Roman world, when a debt had been repaid the certificate of debt was stamped with a single word. This was the Greek word *tetelesthai*. It could best be translated "paid in full." If we put these two pictures together we come up with a beautiful portrait of what Christ accomplished on our behalf on the cross.

On that first Good Friday, Jesus Christ hung from a cross outside the city of Jerusalem. These events took place during the Jewish feast called Passover. As pilgrims went to and from the city, they passed the horrible site of the crucifixion. Wanting to know what hideous crime had been committed that led to such brutal punishment, they would look to the top of the cross to see the written charge against this man. Many surely must have been baffled to read the words "KING OF THE JEWS". From a human perspective this was the reason Jesus was being crucified. It constituted the written charge, or epigraphon, against Him. From God's perspective something quite different was taking place that Friday.

From God's perspective, what was nailed to that cross was our certificate of debt. Christ's epigraphon was actually our cheirographon. This was the reason the

Son of God was hanging on that cross! From noon until three darkness covered the land as cosmic business of incomprehensible significance took place. Finally, there came that moment when Jesus Christ cried out from the cross, "My God, my God, why have you forsaken me?" (Matthew 27:46). In an event that remains one of the great mysteries of the universe, Jesus Christ experienced what He never had known from all eternity: experiential separation from the Father. His cry of agony was followed by a shout of victory. In Matthew's account of these events we are told that "when Jesus had cried out again in a loud voice, he gave up his spirit" (Matthew 27:50). John tells us the content of that cry.

In most of our Bibles we read that Jesus said, "It is finished" (John 19:30). This seems to me an unfortunate translation of the Greek text. In the Greek, Jesus is said to have cried out one single word. Can you guess what it was? *Tetelesthai* was the triumphant cry from the cross. "Paid in full!" This is what Jesus Christ accomplished. As a result of Christ's death, *tetelesthai* now appears emblazoned across your certificate of debt when you appropriate Jesus Christ's atoning death on your behalf through faith. When you and I say yes to Jesus, our certificate of debt is canceled. Our debt has been paid in full. We are forgiven.

It is the finished work of Christ on the cross that makes possible the forgiveness of sin and the removal of all true moral guilt. This is the only adequate (and it is adequate!) solution to the problem of sin and guilt.

FORGIVENESS EXPERIENCED

Once we begin to understand the universal need for forgiveness and how that forgiveness has been made available through Jesus Christ, the logical question becomes, "How can I experience it?" The answer is twofold. There is an initial experience of forgiveness, and an ongoing, day-to-day experience.

The initial experience of forgiveness comes when we personally receive Jesus as Lord and Savior of our lives. In the instant you became a Christian, in the biblical sense of that word, you were forgiven! You were forgiven for past, present, and future sin. Your sin was nailed to the cross with Christ. This amazing moment in our lives is a gift of grace. True moral guilt is removed. This is the starting place in walking in the experience of the cleansing power of Christ.

It usually doesn't take long to recognize that this initial experience of forgiveness needs to be followed by many other experiences of a lesser magnitude. It is imperative for us to understand that every experience of sin and forgiveness throughout our spiritual lives is always rooted in the finished work of Christ. Once we become God's men, our task becomes to learn how to bring the finished work of Christ to bear upon our daily experience. This task requires only three simple steps.

Step One: Confession

The first step in the cleansing process is confession. The Bible says, "If we confess our sins, he is faithful and just and will forgive us our sins" (1 John 1:9). Confession is an act of getting honest with God. The word translated "confess" in 1 John is the Greek word *homologeo*. It literally means "to say the same thing." Confession is a response to the ministry of the Holy Spirit in our lives identifying that we have sinned. When the Holy Spirit convicts, we need to get honest and agree with God that we have in fact "missed the mark."

I have often been asked why we need to confess if all our sin was already forgiven by Christ on the cross. Confession is not for God's benefit. He obviously knows that we have sinned. He also has already provided forgiveness in Christ. Confession is for our benefit. It causes us to squarely face what we have done without excuse, justification, or rationalization.

Part of our daily discipline of time alone with God should include what my friends in AA call a Fearless Moral Inventory. I try to take time every day as I pray to let God show me any area where I need to get honest and experience His forgiveness. I have learned to pray, Lord Jesus, I am a sinner constantly in need of Your grace and the experience of Your forgiveness.

Step Two: Repentance
As we begin to get honest with God, we probably will be forced to recognize that in our sinning we have turned away from God. Repentance is an act whereby we simply turn back to God. The word usually translated repentance is the Greek word *metanoia*. It comes from the verb that means "to change the mind." This change requires an act of the will turning from sin and back to God.

If we are going to be God's men, we need to live a lifestyle of repentance. As soon as we are conscious that we have gotten off the track, we need to change our course. One of the classics of Christian spirituality is a book written by a Russian monk entitled *The Way of the Pilgrim*. In this book, the monk talks about the use of what has become known as the Jesus Prayer. It is a simple little prayer that says, "Lord Jesus Christ, have mercy on me, a sinner." This little prayer (or one very similar to it) will probably be uttered repeatedly by the man who wants to walk with Christ. It is a prayer of repentance.

Step Three: Appropriation

After getting honest with God, and turning back to Him in an attitude of repentance, I am now ready to appropriate the cleansing forgiveness of Jesus Christ. In this step I experientially acknowledge that at the cross, Jesus Christ paid the price for this specific sin. In our hearts, and with our lips, we say, "Thank You, Lord Jesus, that You died for this sin in my life."

As much as I think the Jesus Prayer is a wonderful expression of repentance, I actually think there is a more theologically correct response to the recognition of our sinfulness. The appropriation step reminds me that all my sin has already been forgiven at the cross. A more appropriate response to this reality would be to have a new Jesus Prayer that says, "Lord Jesus Christ, thank You that You have mercy on me, a sinner!" I intend to include this prayer in my own classic of spirituality to be entitled *The Way of the Bozo*.

In the appropriation step we need to open ourselves to Christ and allow Him to cleanse us from the defilement of sin. Like David we pray, "Cleanse me from my sin" (Psalms 51:2). If we take these three steps every time we are conscious that we have sinned, it will be like taking a spiritual shower. We can be clean on the inside and have the freshness in our soul and spirit that a great shower gives our body.

BEYOND FORGIVENESS

When I was a teenager I was envious of a group of my friends who seemed to have this forgiveness thing wired. They were part of a spiritual tradition that believed in a discipline of confession. Every Saturday they would go to church and go through the process of confession with their spiritual leader. Then, having been pronounced forgiven, they would live like hell the rest of the week and head back to church the next Saturday to start the process all over again. At the time I remember thinking that this looked like the best of both worlds. Obviously, once again, I was wrong!

If we have had an authentic experience of repentance and cleansing, our objective ought to be to grow in our relationship with Christ even through our failure and to seek to see change in our lives. Sometimes this will mean assessing whether or not our sin has caused loss to another person and whether or not we need to respond to our forgiveness from God by making restitution where appropriate.

I have seen too many cases where the cause of Christ has actually been damaged by a public testimony concerning the forgiveness of Christ where massive restitution was appropriate, but not undertaken. I always wonder about the person hearing a testimony that goes like this: "I was tremendously wealthy before I met Christ. But God knew that I needed to be humbled to turn to Him, so He let me experience financial disaster and bankruptcy. I'm so glad that I am forgiven now. My life has new meaning." As great as this story might be, often there are seriously damaged relationships behind it. What if in the bankruptcy a former associate lost a great deal of money? He hears the story and thinks, *Great! He's forgiven and I'm out a hundred grand!* Authentic forgiveness requires that whenever possible we seek to make right that which is wrong because of our sin.

To go beyond forgiveness, we need to be willing to open our lives on a daily basis and let God deal with areas of our life that are displeasing to Him. We need to take that daily Fearless Moral Inventory. This is essential if we are going to walk with Christ with a sense of integrity and honesty. The journey with Christ is one of continuous repentance and transformation. My own experience tells me that growth in Christ involves a continual revelation of how "bent" I really am. Any form of spirituality that leads to a sense of self-righteousness is problematic. Authentic spirituality will always lead us to the place where, like the Apostle Paul, we sense that we are the "chief of sinners" (1 Timothy 1:15).

Living with this kind of authenticity and integrity requires that part of our daily walk involves the exercise of certain disciplines which help us stay in a dynamic state of fellowship with Christ. These disciplines are at the heart of step six, a step that will help us grow in our relationship with Christ.

CHECKPOINTS

Personal Reflection
1. Is there any area where you consistently "miss the mark"?
2. What strategy have you used to resolve true moral guilt?
3. Reflect on the meaning of *telelesthai* for your life.

Group Discussion
1. What has your authority been in life?
2. Discuss the error of the "good man" theology.
3. How can you help hold each other accountable for honesty in this area?

6

STEP SIX
GROWING IN CHRIST

Like newborn babies, crave pure spiritual milk,
so that by it you may grow up in your salvation.
(1 Peter 2:2)

*I will seek through prayer, Bible study, and fellowship
to improve my relationship with Christ. On a daily basis
I will seek to know and do the will of God.*

It was an absolutely miserable morning for a race.
The five-mile event was called the Melvin Schoolhouse
Run because the race started and finished at the historic
Melvin Schoolhouse outside of Denver. At five that morn-
ing Bo climbed out of bed and looked out the window. He
was shocked to see six inches of fresh snow on the ground.
One phone call confirmed his worst suspicion: the race
was still on.

Arriving at the schoolhouse, he was amazed to see
how many other men had showed up to plow through
the snow. The starter shot his gun and the crowd was
off through the mush. The first mile of the race was on
hard pavement, and the pace was relatively normal in
spite of the rotten weather conditions. Then everything
went south fast. Suddenly, from halfway back in the pack
Bo could tell that the course headed into a country field.
For the next three miles Bo and his running partner,
Bob, plowed through the snow, climbed over barbed-
wire fences, slogged through creeks, and overcame an

amazing number of obstacles. It was incomprehensible that the race officials would pick this kind of terrain.

Halfway through the open field Bo turned to Bob and announced that he "was not a well person." Bob looked at Bo between fences and creeks and observed that, in fact, Bo was turning a very interesting shade of green. To help ease the pain Bob cheerily suggested, "Wouldn't it be amazing if the lead runner took the wrong turn and the entire field followed him on this wild-goose chase?"

After five grueling miles, and several episodes of tossing his cookies, Bo arrived back at the Melvin Schoolhouse for the awards ceremony. The race organizer stood up with an immense grin on his face and looked out at the totally exhausted runners. The first line out of his mouth went something like this: "I'm really sorry for what you just went through. The lead runner took a wrong turn and led the field off course. You were never supposed to leave the pavement." I looked over at Bo and said, "Someday this will make a great illustration!"

Who you follow sets the course of your life. If the leader of the pack you run with takes a "wrong turn," you will eventually find yourself in big trouble. When you came to know Christ, and started taking the steps contained in this book, you began following a new leader. His name is Jesus Christ and He will never lead you astray. Step six is designed to help you develop a personal strategy for following Him.

GOD'S WILL

Bill was a senior in college when he first heard the good news that there was a personal God who loved him. Part of the message which attracted him to Jesus Christ was the promise that God had a plan for his life. Like many young men in college, the future was filled with uncertainties for Bill. He was graduating with a degree in economics. His plan was to apply to law school in the hopes that some day he could become a corporate attorney. The plan was shaky because Bill lacked a sense of direction. His life seemed confusing. The thought that the living God might have a purpose for his life was very attractive.

Bill committed his life to Christ and began the adventure of seeking to be God's man. Part of his journey involved learning how to discover God's will for his life. Bill soon learned that his expectations of how this would happen were a bit faulty. He thought God would clearly lay out a plan for the next twenty years of his life and that he would know with absolute certainty exactly what to do to realize that plan. It didn't happen quite that way.

Bill began to discover that God's plan for his life unfolded day by day as he grew in his relationship with Jesus Christ. Bill was thinking of God's plan in terms of specific daily actions without realizing that those daily activities always occur within the context of our personal growth. He began to understand that there is a framework of spiritual principles that governs all specific issues of guidance. The primary dynamic of this framework is the dynamic of relationship.

THE RELATIONAL DYNAMIC

God has a plan for your life, too. The overriding principle which will guide that plan is the fact that God is more concerned with who you are than with what you do. God's basic will for your life is revealed in the New Testament book of Romans where the Apostle Paul teaches that God has predestined that you become conformed to the image of His Son (Romans 8:29). All the specifics of God's plan for your life will always move you closer to this primary objective.

A life committed to walking with Christ can be extremely rewarding and fulfilling. It also has the potential to be unbelievably frustrating and discouraging. Our desire to live as God's men is rooted in a mind-set filled with good intentions. Most men have good intentions. I have never known a man who entered marriage with the desire to have his marriage fail. I have never met a man who started his family with the intention of neglecting or abusing his children. Most of the men I have known over the years have expressed the desire to have healthy and vital friendships. And yet . . . marriages fail, families crumble, friendships disintegrate, and the desperate needs of the world remain largely unaddressed.

At the same time, I do know men who have vital marriages, healthy families, meaningful friendships, and who are making a significant difference in the quality of life on the planet because of their selfless contribution of time, talent, and resources. Both groups have good intentions. The difference between these two groups is often a matter of whether or not a man develops a vital relationship with Jesus Christ. Apart from the dynamic of this relationship, our lives will often be powerless and chaotic, even when our intentions are good. Don't misunderstand what I am saying; religion will not make this happen. Only a vital relationship will do.

Religion Versus Relationship
Religious men can be the most miserable men in the world. Religious men are often angry, resentful, critical, self-righteous, pseudopious, and boring. Religious men live lives filled with "shoulds" and "oughts" and

rules and regulations. Religious men can even use their religious systems to hide their own personal neuroses and insanity. Religious men crucified Jesus Christ. In making these statements I need to clarify what I mean by the term *religious*.

Religion is man's attempt to reach God and appease Him with human effort. Authentic, biblical spirituality is not a religion. Authentic, biblical spirituality is primarily a relationship. It is rooted in what God has already accomplished on our behalf through the finished work of Christ. The primary theological distinctive separating biblical spirituality from every other religious system, including some claiming to be Christian, is the principle of grace.

Grace is unmerited favor. Because of grace, our relationship with God is a gift, freely given. "It is by grace you have been saved, through faith—and this not from yourselves, it is a gift of God—not by works" (Ephesians 2:8-9). A proper understanding of grace leads to relationship. Without grace, spirituality disintegrates into religion.

Jesus Christ came to offer men a relationship with God. Do you remember which group opposed Him with the greatest resistance? A religious sect called the Pharisees. The Pharisees, in general, seemed to suffer from a unique form of neurotic self-deception we call self-righteousness. Their spirituality involved an amazing system of human works. They were resistant to grace because they imagined they didn't need it.

On the other hand, the prostitutes, the tax collectors, and assorted other social outcasts were highly receptive to grace. They knew that if authentic spirituality were based on good behavior, they didn't have a chance! When grace was extended they jumped at the opportunity and entered into relationship with Christ.

Much of what passes for Christianity today bears a tragic resemblance to the legalism of the Pharisees. The Church Lady of "Saturday Night Live" was not created in a vacuum. My hunch is that she is probably the product of the writer's negative experience with a Christian Pharisee.

When a man has a vital relationship with Jesus Christ, he will bear very little resemblance to the Church Lady. Jesus Christ is challenging and exciting! He was and is the most attractive and winsome personality in all of human history. It is mind-boggling to think that He desires to have a relationship with you and me.

Relationships influence the course of our lives. We tend to become like the men we spend time with. How we think, feel, look, and behave are all influenced by those with whom we are in significant relationship. Several years ago I learned a humorous lesson about this principle.

A group of men from our church invited a group of our nonchurch buddies to join us on a cross-country, mid-life crisis motorcycle trip. The plan was to fly to Milwaukee, Wisconsin, the birthplace of Harley-Davidson motorcycles, and ride cross country back to Denver via the Black Hills and Yellowstone National Park.

Our group was composed of white-collar professionals and business executives. Among the professions represented were lawyers, dentists, pastors, real estate developers, and psychologists. Under normal circumstances these men are usually found wearing suits and ties in the marketplace. At their most casual you might find them in khakis and polo shirts on the golf course. During this two-week adventure I witnessed an amazing transformation.

The night before we left Denver to fly to Milwaukee

we gathered with our wives for a send-off dinner and party. The invitation suggested we wear appropriate motorcycling attire. I'm sure Norm and Joan's neighbors, in the fashionable Green Oaks area of Littleton, Colorado, wondered what was happening to their property values as carload after carload of men and women in worn-out jeans, black T-shirts, and black leather jackets entered the house. There was only one hopeful-looking arrival in the group: me!

Most of the men going on the adventure were picking up new Harleys in Milwaukee to ride on the trip. I was part of a minority of five who were shipping our non-Harley motorcycles by truck. I decided that my attire for the party needed to reflect the fact that I would be riding a BMW motorcycle on the trip. I walked into this den of black leather wearing a tuxedo jacket, tuxedo shirt, cummerbund, and black tie. The outfit was highlighted by a pair of Big Dog shorts and Polo slippers. I immediately identified myself as the official trip yuppie!

What started as a joke eventually took on a reality of its own. Over the next week and a half I watched a group of men go through a minor metamorphosis. I would be heading down the highway with several other non-Harley riders, cruising along at fifty-five miles per hour, when suddenly a group of the toughest-looking guys you have ever seen would blow by us like we were standing still. Unshaven, without helmets, bandannas covering their heads, these guys struck fear into the hearts of defenseless women and children. Then it hit me: It was our group! They were becoming bonafide bikers! The "biker" relationships were shaping and reinforcing the "biker" behavior.

Relationships shape our lives. For that reason you and I need to "hang out" with Jesus Christ. Our relationship with Christ will positively shape the course of our lives and provide the empowerment necessary to become God's men. Step six requires a commitment on our part to develop the necessary disciplines that enhance our relationship with Christ. These disciplines will help us "hang out" with Christ and learn to know Him and how to follow Him.

CULTIVATING A RELATIONSHIP WITH CHRIST

How do you cultivate a relationship with Christ? At this point a very important assumption is being made. Somewhere along the line you were challenged to make a personal decision to ask Jesus Christ to come into your life. You made a commitment to embrace Christ as both Savior and Lord of life. Without this commitment all attempts to cultivate an authentic spiritual life will prove frustrating and futile.

In chapter 3 this initial transaction with Jesus Christ was illustrated in the following manner:

What does it mean to have Jesus in our hearts? The heart is a symbol of the innermost, immaterial center of our being. In every moment of our day, in every decision we make and every action we take, someone sits enthroned at the heart of our being. The throne is either occupied by Christ or self. The illustration on the left is a picture of a man's life before making the decision of step two. Self rules the heart; Christ is outside the life. The man on the right illustrates one who has received Christ. Personal, spiritual conversion is a matter of dethroning self (the essence of the biblical mandate to repent) and inviting Christ into our lives to occupy this position of lordship or control.

Cultivating our relationship with Christ will require a vigilance on our part to maintain Christ's reign in our inner life. In step four we saw that when we assert our self-will in opposition to God's will, the illustration of the man on the right is distorted to look like this:

CHRIST DETHRONED

Christ is still in his life, but the relationship has been distorted. Ego or self has assumed the place of influence only the Spirit should occupy. Cultivation of a vital and healthy spiritual life involves the exercise of certain important disciplines which help keep self dethroned and Christ enthroned.

THE BASIC DISCIPLINES

Because God loves us, He has provided a number of resources to facilitate the vitality of our relationship with

Christ. These resources are activated through the exercise of the basic disciplines. There are four areas in which discipline needs to be developed if the spiritual growth process is to provide the empowerment necessary to become the men God intends us to be. All four areas and their corresponding disciplines have the objective of helping us grow in our relationship with Christ.

The Bible

Communication is a critical component in every relationship. If we are to have an authentic relationship with God, we need to experience a special process of communication. God has spoken. He spoke through the prophets, the apostles, and His Son, all of whose messages have been recorded for us on the pages of the world's most unique book. It is called the Bible. No other book in all the world is like it. It is a "living and active" book (Hebrews 4:12). Through this book God continues to speak. That is why it is often called the Word of God. It is a powerful vehicle that plays a central role in our relationship with Christ.

To have a vital, productive, and effective spiritual life, it is imperative that we develop a consistent time of interacting with the Bible. For many men, setting aside time in the morning to read and reflect on the Bible has proven to be an invaluable resource in cultivating their relationship with Christ.

Over time, as this relationship matures, we will sense God communicating with us as we attend to His Word. As we seek to grow in our ability to be Christ's men, the Bible becomes our manual, containing the blueprint for meaning and significance.

When I first committed my life to Christ, I was skeptical about reading or studying the Bible. On sev-

eral occasions before becoming a Christian I had picked
up a *King James Version* of the Bible and started out on
page 1. It didn't take long before I found myself bogged
down in some obscure genealogy. The book just didn't
seem that exciting or relevant. After my encounter with
Christ I received two very good pieces of advice about
the Bible.

First, I was encouraged to obtain a copy of a modern
translation. If the *King James Version* seems archaic to you,
it is probably because the *King James Version is* archaic. I
know that for many old saints who have been reading the
Bible for years, there is something quite reverent about the
"thees" and "thous" of the King James. What many people don't understand is that this was simply the language
of the common people at the time this version was translated out of the ancient texts. If you are just beginning
your journey with Christ, you will find that using one of
the many good modern translations of the Bible will help
immensely. I personally use the *New International Version*.
A friendly clerk at your local Christian bookstore would
be glad to help you find a version that you find readable
and enjoyable.

The second tip is this: Start in the New Testament.
Don't get me wrong. Eventually you will find the Old
Testament fascinating and extremely helpful. To get off
to a good start, begin by reading one of the four gospels.
The gospels contain the historical narratives of the life and
teaching of Jesus. Start with Matthew or Luke and then
head on to John. Begin by reading a chapter a day. You
will find that this simple discipline radically improves the
quality of your spiritual life.

As you read, ask the Holy Spirit to open your spiritual eyes to see and your spiritual ears to hear what
God is saying to you (Psalm 119:18). Sometimes His

message will come clearly through the words of the text. For instance, you might be struggling in your relationship with your wife when you run across Ephesians 5:25: "Husbands, love your wives, just as Christ loved the church." God's message is clear. As a man who is following Christ, you need to love your wife as Christ loved the Church. Now you have to make a decision about how you are going to put the message into action today.

At other times the Holy Spirit might use the Bible in a more mystical way. You could be reading about how Jesus loved Lazarus when suddenly you have the sense that God is saying to you, "I love you like that!" At other times there might not be a specific message, but as you read the Bible you will have the sense that Christ is near you and with you. There is no substitute for developing this discipline.

Over time you will learn that there are a variety of "delivery systems" for God's Word. At times you will simply *hear* the Word as someone like your pastor speaks on Sunday. At times you might *read* through large sections of the Bible as you would an exciting novel. As you begin to grow you will probably find yourself wanting to understand the Bible at a more significant level, so you will begin to *study* it like a textbook. Your study might become so exciting that you find a verse or a passage that you want to *memorize* so that you can always have it with you. When God begins to speak to you through the Bible, you will find yourself stopping to contemplate and reflect on what you are hearing. This is the practice of biblical *meditation*. These five delivery systems will help you get a handle on God's Word. The classic illustration of how these five work together looks like this:

THE HAND ILLUSTRATION

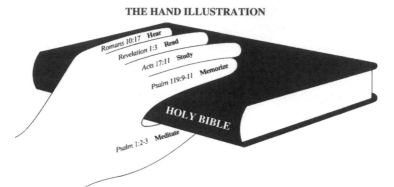

Finally, you want to be a "doer" and not just a "hearer" of the Word (James 1:22). You should find yourself desiring to put into action the guidance God has given you. As you exercise this discipline of the spiritual walk, you will begin to discover that you are growing in your ability to understand God's will for your life.

Prayer

Through reading, studying, and memorizing the Bible, God speaks to us. But communication is a two-way process. We also need to speak to God. Through prayer we have been given this privilege. Along with time spent in the Bible, time in prayer is an essential means of enhancing our relationship with Christ.

Prayer is a form of communication with God. In prayer we move into a conscious experience of the presence of God. For many of us this means of growing in our spiritual life does not come naturally. We need to learn how to enjoy a more meaningful experience of prayer. Like the disciples, we have the need to come to Jesus and ask Him to teach us to pray (Luke 11:1).

In response to this request Jesus gave the disciples a sevenfold pattern of prayer. Most of us are probably familiar with the Lord's Prayer as a rote, memorized, liturgical prayer. When used as an outline of seven topics, the prayer provides a helpful guide for developing a more meaningful prayer life. For more extensive help in this area you might want to pick up a copy of my book *Transforming Your Prayer Life*. For our purposes let me briefly explore the seven components:

1. *Relationship*—"Father"—Prayer begins with a time of focusing on God as our heavenly Father and consciously entering His presence.
2. *Worship*—"Hallowed be Your name"—Prayer is a time to set our minds and hearts on the nature of God and give Him praise and thanksgiving for who He is and what He does.
3. *Intervention*—"Your kingdom come . . ."—In prayer we have been given the privilege of appropriating God's intervention in our lives. As we relinquish our self-will to His will, we can pray that the realities of His Kingdom would influence our personal lives, our families, our churches, our nation, and the world.
4. *Provision*—"Give us this day . . ."—With Christ as the highest priority of our lives we are able to pray with confidence for God's provision. During prayer we set before the Father our needs, our desires, and all sources of anxiety in our lives.
5. *Forgiveness*—"Forgive us our sins . . ."—Prayer is a time of getting honest with God. It is a time to wrestle with our flaws and failures and allow the grace of God to touch our lives with the cleansing work of Christ. In prayer we can take a fearless moral inventory of our lives and get back on track with God's will and His plans.

6. *Protection*—"Lead us not . . . deliver us . . ."—Living a spiritual life is a battle. We need protection from our own susceptibility to temptation and also from the hostile spiritual forces that seek to harm us. In prayer we can appropriate the leading of the Spirit and the protection of the Father.
7. *Affirmation*—"Yours is the kingdom . . ."—We close our time of prayer with a series of affirmations regarding God's sovereign authority over our lives.

Over time, as we grow in our personal prayer experience, many other dimensions of prayer can be added to this pattern. This pattern is simply designed to help us begin to practice a discipline of prayer that will put us in touch with Christ on a daily basis.

King David was one of the great men of the Bible. Like you and me he lived a very busy and full life. He was the leader of Israel's army and the ruler of the people. His life was filled with many of the same challenges and difficulties we face daily. Yet, David could say, "I am a man of prayer" (Psalm 109:4). David enjoyed an amazing relationship with God. Reading through the book of Psalms, you realize that here was a man's man who had a unique level of intimacy with God. Nothing is more significant in developing that kind of intimacy than learning how to pray and becoming a man of prayer.

Fellowship
You might conceptualize the resources of the Bible and prayer as direct, vertical means of developing our relationship with God. There are also horizontal resources available which provide additional means of facilitating our spiritual growth. Fellowship encompasses all those

relationships we enjoy with our fellow travelers on the spiritual journey. In fellowship, we experience the reality of Christ's love as it is expressed through tangible, human vehicles. Authentic fellowship enhances our relationship with Christ.

Tim was by nature a loner. He never had many friends and certainly none that really knew him well. He committed his life to Christ while watching a Billy Graham crusade on television. For several months after his commitment he tried to get to know Christ on his own. Eventually, he began to feel like something was missing.

One night he was walking through his living room when the theme song from "Cheers" was playing on the television. The words hit him hard: "Sometimes you want to go where everybody knows your name, and they're always glad you came . . . you want to be where everybody knows your name." Suddenly, Tim knew what was missing. He needed some other men to accompany him on his journey with Christ.

Tim found a church in his neighborhood that had an active men's Bible study group. Through the group he met several other men who invited him to become part of a small support group. The group was working through The Navigators' 2:7 program. The fellowship of this group was exactly what Tim needed. God began to work in Tim's life through the care and friendship of these few men, and in turn, God began to work through Tim to minister to them.

Fellowship rarely happens without some action on our part. It requires a commitment of time, energy, and resources. The cost of working at developing these relationships is far outweighed by the benefits. In fellowship we encounter Christ through His Body. It is a great gift of God that is essential in the challenge of becoming God's man.

Witness

Witness encompasses all our relationships of life with men and women who are not yet on the spiritual journey. The last challenge Jesus Christ gave His men before He ascended to the Father was to be His witnesses in all the world (Acts 1:8). He actually told them, "You will be my witnesses." We often think of witnessing as something we do. Again, primarily, witnessing is something we are. To be a witness is to be a reflection of the reality that we know and follow Christ. This is where the rubber meets the road.

Having taken the first six steps, we "move out" with step seven. This step helps us understand how to be an effective witness. We will look at this step in the next chapter.

THE WHEEL

Before the rubber meets the road, let's take a look at what the basic disciplines look like when you put them all together. The classic illustration of these disciplines is the Navigator Wheel:

The four disciplines form the spokes on the wheel. The vertical spokes represent the means of direct communication with Christ. Through the Word, or the Bible, God speaks to us. Through prayer we speak to God. Communication is established and relationship is enhanced.

The horizontal spokes represent indirect means of relating to God. Fellowship puts us in relationship with other men who are learning the Christian walk. We are on a team. The spiritual journey is an epic adventure. We walk arm in arm and side by side. Through the brothers we experience the love and support of Christ in a tangible way. The final spoke of the wheel is the witness spoke. We become living vehicles through whom Christ lives His life in the world.

At the center of the wheel is the hub: Christ Himself. All the disciplines serve to cultivate our relationship with Him. As He is at the center of our lives and we are in dynamic relationship with Him, we are ready to hit the pavement and be His men in our homes, in our neighborhoods, at our jobs, in the city, and around the world. Having spent time in step six growing in Christ, we are now ready to take step seven.

CHECKPOINTS

Personal Reflection

1. Which of the two illustrations on page 98 most represents your life?
2. How consistent is your time in the Word? What could you do to improve in this area of basic spiritual discipline?
3. Spend ten minutes daily this week praying through the seven components of the Lord's Prayer.

Group Discussion
1. Discuss the signs of self taking over the throne.
2. How does prayer help keep Christ at the center?
3. Share your strongest and weakest spoke on the wheel.

7

STEP SEVEN
SERVING THE KINGDOM

You will be my witnesses.
(Acts 1:8)

*Lord Jesus, by Your grace and with Your help I will
seek to be Your witness in my home, in my
neighborhood, in my workplace, and in the world.
Live Your life through me today.*

I am one of the luckiest guys in the world! Actually, luck
has nothing to do with it. I have been richly blessed and
I am immensely and eternally grateful for God's blessing
in my life. Two of the greatest sources of His blessing are
my teenage daughter, Stephanie, and my seven-year-old
son, Baker. This has been a very important year in our
family. I will remember it as the year my daughter fell in
love with boys and my son fell in love with baseball. One
of these new realities is giving me ulcers and the other
has brought great joy to my life. Can you guess which is
which?

Baker's love of baseball began with the enthusiasm
that swept Denver upon the arrival of major league baseball. My seven-year-old is already a dyed-in-the-wool
Rockies fan. Baker's birthday is April 9. That also happened to be the day of the first home game the Rockies
ever played in Denver. For his birthday Baker wanted
tickets to this game. Since April 9 was also Good Friday this year, and since tickets were going for about

$250 bucks a pop, we didn't make the opener. However, through the generosity of a friend, we were fifteen rows back between third base and home plate on April 10. It was a gorgeous day in Denver and the Rockies even defeated the Montreal Expos.

There is only one activity Baker likes more than watching baseball, and that is playing baseball. I am having a blast teaching my son how to catch, throw, and bat. We spend hours out in the yard playing ball. This week his big moment has finally arrived. He takes the field in the real thing: YMCA coach-pitch baseball. As I think about this momentous occasion I keep hearing the words every one of us has probably uttered at some point in our personal athletic career: "Put me in, Coach!"

Some of the most frustrating minutes of my life were spent sitting on the bench while some other guy was on the field playing my position. Finally, I could stand it no longer. Bolting from the bench, I dropped to my knees while pulling on the coach's pant leg: "Put me in, Coach!"

I was lucky. I actually was able to play a good portion of most games in which I competed. But, I remember the unlucky guys who spent most of their time on the bench. I observed two kinds of guys who sat the bench most of their athletic careers. One type of guy longed to get in the game but lacked the ability to make a significant contribution. I admired these guys. They wanted to play so badly that they were willing to endure the hard work of practice knowing that the probability of getting in the game depended on our team either blowing the other team out so thoroughly that the bench squad could take the field, or our team getting blown out so badly that the coach threw in the towel by putting in the bench brigade. When the coach finally shouted something like "Smedley, get in there!" a look of wild ecstasy filled their faces as they charged onto the field.

The other type of guy actually liked sitting the bench. Practice was their life. They liked suiting up for the games, but the thought of actually playing terrified them. I have to admit, I could never understand this mentality. Unfortunately, it is possible to be this same type of man when it comes to following Christ. Far too many men are experts at "practice" but never take the field. Someone has observed that the work of the Kingdom of Christ is much like an NFL game.

I live in Denver, Colorado. I love the Denver Broncos. Every once in a while, a friend or member of our church offers my family a set of the most coveted item in Denver on a Sunday afternoon in the fall: Bronco tickets! It is tough to beat the excitement of sitting in Mile High Stadium when the Broncos are in the heat of battle. If you stopped in the fourth quarter of most any Bronco game to wax philosophical, you might realize that what you are observing is seventy-five thousand men and women desperately in need of exercise watching twenty-two men desperately in need of rest! That, sadly, is often an accurate metaphor of what is happening in the Kingdom of Christ. Too few do too much, while too many do too little. Too many men are sitting on the bench. God is looking for a few good men, too! He is looking for men who will shout with great enthusiasm, "Put me in, Coach!"

SERVING THE KINGDOM

How would you like to know the secret of lasting happiness? How would you like to have a deep sense of joy and fulfillment that does not depend on your external circumstances or the acquisition of the latest gadget? How would you like to be sure that your life is counting for something significant? The answers to these questions lie in a proper understanding of how to take step seven and begin to get in the game and serve the Kingdom of Christ.

During his "Christian" phase, Bob Dylan recorded an album entitled *Slow Train Coming*. One of the songs on that album reminded the listener that "you've gotta serve somebody." In very un-Dylanesque fashion, Mr. Zimmerman (Dylan's real name) went right to the heart of the matter and proclaimed that "it might be the Devil, or it might be the Lord, but you've gotta serve somebody." We might not agree with the bipolar evaluation Dylan made, but the primary message of the song is without question. Life is about serving. The object of our service and the product of our serving will, to a great extent, determine whether our lives are fulfilled and significant, or shallow and meaningless.

Who is the happiest man who ever lived on the planet? Apart from Jesus Christ, whom the Bible says was anointed "with the oil of joy" above all his companions (Hebrews 1:9, quoting Psalm 45:7), it might have been a young Italian lad by the name of Frank.

Growing up in a wealthy home, Frank enjoyed all the advantages wealth could buy. He lived to be served. One day, while on a trip to Rome, he had an experience with God which started a process of transformation in his life. He sensed Christ calling him to "Come, follow Me." Frank responded to the call of God on his life. In effect he said, "Put me in, Coach!" Unlike the rich young ruler of Jesus' day, Frank gave away all his worldly possessions and followed Christ in absolute material poverty. His material impoverishment led to great spiritual prosperity. He spent the remainder of his life, like Jesus, seeking not to be served, but to serve (Mark 10:45). The year was AD 1205 and Frank's full name was Francesco. He lived in the city of Assisi. We know him today as Saint Francis of Assisi. He is perhaps best known for his constant prayer to God, "Make me an instrument of your peace." In other words, "Put me in, Coach!"

The great passion of Saint Francis' life was to be an instrument of God's peace. In the Sermon on the Mount Jesus taught the disciples, "Blessed are the peacemakers" (Matthew 5:9). Peacemaking is rooted in the Hebrew concept of peace. The Hebrew word for peace is *shalom*. Shalom was much more than a greeting in the world of the Old Testament. It was a word that captured the essence of what a relationship with God could bring to a life. Peace, in the biblical sense, has a much broader meaning than our limited use of this word.

When we use the word *peace* we are often referring to the end of hostility. In the sixties many of us learned to flash two fingers in the air and chant, "Peace!" This routine expressed the desire of a generation to see the war in Vietnam come to an end. In the nineties, as the tanks of Desert Shield became the weapons of Desert Storm, the whole world longed for peace in the Middle East.

Although shalom includes the idea of the end of hostility, it is a much more comprehensive concept. The experience of shalom in the Bible is intimately related to God's blessing. Shalom was a multidimensional reality that included material prosperity, physical health, emotional contentment, relational harmony, and spiritual salvation. Shalom is a state of total well-being flowing from a proper relationship with God. It is a word that speaks of the quality of life that all men and women long to experience. Our role in dispensing shalom is a critical component of becoming God's men.

MEN OF ACTION

Step seven is a step of action. It is a step in which we take all the resources brought to bear on our lives by the first six steps and move out into the world as a witness for Christ. It is the step in which we allow Christ in us to live His life through us in tangible ways. A witness is a peacemaker. A peacemaker is a man of action.

Because of the multidimensional nature of *shalom*, peacemaking encompasses a wide variety of possible activities. Peacemaking is an attempt to be an instrument of God's *shalom*. It requires that we use the physical, emotional, spiritual, relational, financial, and political resources at our disposal to improve the quality of another human being's life. Peacemaking is the tangible expression of loving our neighbor (Matthew 22:39).

Becoming a peacemaker requires a fundamental shift in a man's value system. Our cultural paradigm indoctrinates us with a subconscious message to "Love things; use people." If we are going to get serious about being God's men, we must experience a paradigm shift that motivates us to "Love people; use things." This is the underlying philosophical value system of the man of God. It is the life philosophy of a peacemaker.

Peacemaking can take many different forms. Some of us have the ability to be physical peacemakers. By that I mean we can use part of our time, energy, and resources to improve the physical quality of another person's life. Others are better equipped to be emotional peacemakers. Some will be used by God to be spiritual peacemakers. God has uniquely created each of us to play a peacemaking role in our world.

Every Tuesday evening a beautiful thing happens at Cherry Hills Community Church. The church is located in the wealthy Cherry Hills area bordering the city of Denver. It would be easy for a church like this to forget about the needs of the poor. But on Tuesday evenings Manna Ministries opens its doors. Originally started as a food bank, Manna now offers food, clothing, medical care, and even free haircuts to families in southern Denver who are in need of a little physical *shalom*. The men who volunteer their time at Manna are peacemakers, putting their faith in Christ into action.

The stately governor's mansion of the state of Colorado sits on one corner of Eighth Avenue and Logan Street in Denver, Colorado. Across the street from the governor's pad stands an exciting model of peacemaking. It is called Providence House. Providence House is a residential "lifeboat" for homeless people in transition. Many homeless people in America don't fit the stereotype of someone on welfare. Some are hardworking victims of life's unforeseen hardships. Many need a little *shalom* to get back on their feet. Under the leadership of Bo Mitchell, a men's ministry called Executive Network was formed to tap into the giving power of Denver's executive community in order to liberate the resources necessary to provide a place like Providence House. Every man involved in the project gets the blessing of being a peacemaker.

Sometimes the challenges of serving the Kingdom require more than physical peacemaking. Dale Hudson and his wife, Alice, are two of my heroes. For over ten years Dale and Alice have opened their home to foster children. During this period of time over thirty children have found a temporary home with the Hudsons. Sensitized to the needs of handicapped children through their daughter Dusty's struggle with cerebral palsy, many of the Hudsons' "kids" have had unique needs that others have been unwilling to meet. Not only have Dale and Alice provided a physical home, they have loved and nurtured these children emotionally as well. Miracles happen in the Hudson home. A few "hopeless cases" have graduated from college and are living productive lives because the Hudsons have been dispensers of emotional *shalom*.

Rich Beach is a peacemaker. For over twenty years I have seen a nearly endless stream of spiritually destitute men find new meaning in life through Rich's efforts in the area of spiritual peacemaking. With a winsome personality and genuine concern, it is usually only a matter of minutes into almost any conversation before Rich raises the question of a man's spiritual condition. His sensitive boldness opens multitudes of doors. Where need and openness are present, Rich tastefully shares how to have a relationship with Jesus Christ. In restaurants, on airplanes, at shopping centers, and in nearly every imaginable arena of life, Rich leads people to Christ. The deepest spiritual needs of men and women are brought in touch with the *shalom* of God.

Bill Armstrong is a peacemaker. For eighteen years he served the people of Colorado, first in Congress and then for twelve years in the United States Senate. During all those years Bill sought to use his political influence to improve the quality of life of countless men and women. His motivation was his love for Christ and people.

Tom Weins is a peacemaker. By day he is the aggressive CEO of Environmental Recovery Systems. By winter night you can find Tom distributing gloves and blankets under the viaducts of downtown Denver to homeless men and women.

Rich Valenziano is a peacemaker. As a family physician he has committed his life to serving the medical needs of hurting people. But on Sunday mornings he gives his time and energy to teach five-year-old children about Jesus.

Flip Cole is a peacemaker. He spends his days building swimming pools in back yards. But on Tuesday nights he gives his time and emotional energy to build relationships with clinically schizophrenic street people at the Network coffee house.

Mike Anderson is a peacemaker. Hour by hour, day by day, he pours his life into being an instrument of shalom in the broken, fragmented, disillusioned, and distressed lives of the people who come through the doors of his counseling office.

These are the real heroes of our world. They are the hidden saints who improve the quality of life on our planet for countless multitudes. They are the peacemakers. They are men who have a vital relationship with Christ that is expressed by their service to the Kingdom of Christ. Most of them are not much different from you and me. They have limited time and resources. Their weeks contain only seven days. Their mortgages are due on the first of the month. Their cars break down and their children need braces. So how do they do it? The answer lies in understanding that inside the value system of every peacemaker you will find a commitment to serving Christ by being His witness in the world.

BECOMING A PEACEMAKER

I have not shared the preceding illustrations in the hope that you would admire these men from afar. I have shared these stories to challenge you to become a peacemaker. "Who, me?" Yes, you! You were designed and created to be an instrument of *shalom* in the world.

The Chinese character for the word *crisis* is a combination of two other Chinese characters. One is the character for danger, and the other is the character for opportunity. Our world is in a state of crisis. Our nation is in a state of crisis. Our cities are in crisis; our neighborhoods are in crisis; and often, our own families and lives are in crisis. We are surrounded by crisis. Crisis creates challenge because with the danger of crisis come the opportunities crisis creates for peacemaking.

Never in human history have there been more opportunities to be a witness for Christ. The danger most men face is becoming so overwhelmed by the scope of the need that they do nothing. In order to become effective as witnesses, we need to sort through the multitude of opportunities available and focus our limited time, energy, and resources where we can make our greatest peacemaking contribution. It is not enough to "visualize world peace." The seven-step process requires us to become proactive in the peacemaking process. In order to help accomplish this task, it will be necessary for us to set our priorities, discover our gifts, identify our passion, and seek to understand God's call on our lives.

Setting Your Priorities

Jake was a successful young businessman. Successful, that is, by the standards set by our fallen culture. He had poured his life into building a business that had enabled him to own a beautiful home, drive a great car, and join an exclusive country club. Along the way he had nearly destroyed his marriage and missed many of the joys of being actively involved in raising his own children. Jake had a problem with priorities.

Through the influence of a friend, Jake was invited to attend an overnight retreat at Eagle's Nest Ranch outside of Denver. Even though Jake suspected it was going to be "religious," he went because Eagle's Nest was owned by Philip Anschutz, one of the most successful business-men in the United States. What Jake didn't know was that God was going to shake him to the core in the next eighteen hours.

For a day and a half Jake listened to a series of messages on the subject of relationships and priorities. He was given a glimpse of the way God designed life. It didn't take long for Jake to see that his priorities were far from consistent with God's.

I am always amazed to see how God touches a life. At the end of our retreat, Jake approached me with tears in his eyes. God had laid hold of him. Months later he would write to tell me how those few hours at Eagle's Nest had changed his life. He began to live by a new set of priorities.

THE LADDER OF LOVE

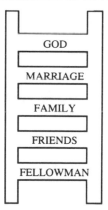

GOD

MARRIAGE

FAMILY

FRIENDS

FELLOWMAN

Over the last twelve years, as I have had the privilege of teaching about God's priorities, I have met a lot of "Jakes": men who needed a tool to help set godly priorities. The tool I use is called the Ladder of Love. It is a simple way to visualize the set of relational priorities Jesus established for men who would follow Him.

Jake had never read the Bible. As he started the adventure of becoming God's man he felt overwhelmed with all the information contained in the Book. Many men feel just like Jake. One day a man came to Jesus and asked the best question anyone ever asked the Son of God. This man happened to be a Jewish scribe. A scribe was an expert in the Law of the Old Testament. I think he might have been feeling as overwhelmed as Jake felt when he asked Jesus, "Which is the greatest commandment?" (Matthew 22:36). I sometimes paraphrase this question as, "If you take this whole big book and boil it down to one central principle, what would it be?"

In response to this question Jesus responded, "'Love the Lord your God with all your heart and with all your soul and with all your mind.' This is the first and greatest commandment. And the second is like it: 'Love your neighbor as yourself'" (Matthew 22:37-39). Then Jesus added, "All the Law and the Prophets hang on these two commandments." Jesus was saying that everything God has made known to us in the Bible is simply amplification of understanding and applying these two commands.

Life was designed to be about love. Love is about relationships. If we are going to build our life on the foundation of Christ and His Word, we need a working set of relational priorities. The highest priority of life needs to be our relationship with Christ. He occupies the top rung on the ladder. The greatest (most important) command is to love God. I think you could also add to that statement its corollary: and let God love you.

Love for God, if authentic, will be reflected in love for our neighbor. The rest of the ladder reflects the biblical order of priorities of the various "neighbors" in our lives. For those of us who are married, our wives are to be the highest-priority neighbor next to Christ. This is where peacemaking needs to begin. Our homes are the laboratories God has designed to teach us to love and to serve. Step seven begins with our commitment to love our wives as Christ loved the church.

For those of us who have children, they are to be the next priority after our wives. If we are going to live in conformity with the divine design, we will need to work at giving the proper attention, time, and energy to loving and serving our children. Whenever I speak on the subject of developing biblical priorities, I share ideas about how to tackle this challenge. One of the tips I give is the idea that we need to be thinking that when we come home from work, we actually begin the most important work of our day.

The next rung on the ladder is the "Friend" rung. This rung reflects the fellowship dimension of the Wheel illustration in step six. Fellowship needs to become a priority in our lives. We need to make a small group of brothers a central part of serving Christ in the world.

The final rung on the ladder is the "Fellowman" rung. Here we place opportunities for loving and serving men and women who live in a fallen world. By placing this rung on the ladder we are saying that people are more important than things.

This little tool, and the relational commitment it represents, is a mental "filter" through which we can process our lives. It can serve as a quick check in every decision and action we take. When faced with a tough decision we simply ask, "How does this fit with my Ladder of Love?" Quickly we can picture the ladder and assess the decision in terms of how it affects our relationship with God, our wife, our children, our brothers in Christ, and our fellowman. If the decision enhances these relationships, it is a good decision. If the decision is in conflict with these priorities, we probably should stop and think carefully about its implications before proceeding.

Having established biblical priorities, we then need to know how we can make our most significant peacemaking contribution. This decision might seem overwhelming. A few more steps need to be taken to sharpen the focus of our serving commitment.

Discovering Your Gifts

The call to peacemaking is not intended to be a call to attempt to do something you cannot do. It is intended to be a response to a task you have been custom-equipped to accomplish. When you made the spiritual commitment of receiving Christ, many wonderful transactions took place in your life. You were invaded! Christ came to live in you by means of the person of the Holy Spirit. When the Holy Spirit invaded your life, He endowed you with supernatural abilities the Bible calls spiritual gifts. The Bible says, "He gives them to each one, just as he determines" (1 Corinthians 12:11). The spiritual gifts God has given you will enable you to effectively accomplish the peacemaking tasks you are intended to accomplish.

Four different passages in the New Testament relate to this subject of spiritual gifts: Romans 12:1-8, 1 Corinthians 12–14, Ephesians 4:7-16, 1 Peter 4:10-11. In these passages nineteen different spiritual gifts are identified. Every man who has received Christ possesses one or more of these gifts. Part of the process of spiritual growth involves the discovery and development of our gifts. Many churches have programs designed to help you discover your spiritual gifts.

One of the great tragedies of the contemporary church has been its failure to carefully place gifted people in the ministries where they belong. Often, the mission of the church has been carried out on the "warm body" principle. If you need a Sunday school teacher, you find a warm body and fill the position. How many little boys and girls have had boring and irrelevant Sunday experiences because their teachers, as well-intentioned as they might have been, had no teaching gifts? When you discover your gifts, you will have come a long way toward narrowing the focus of how you can best be a peacemaker.

Identifying Your Passion

Willow Creek Community Church in South Barrington, Illinois, has developed an excellent program to help its members discover where to invest their energies in making a significant contribution for the Kingdom of Christ. Along with helping men and women discover their spiritual gifts, Willow Creek also helps people identify their passion in ministry. The underlying assumption of this dimension of the church's Network ministry is the belief that God gives us a passion for what He has created us to accomplish.

Our passion is intimately related to our person. Like the snowflake, no two men on the planet are identical. Every man is an expression of the creative genius of God. We might warp and distort the beauty, but our uniqueness remains intact. King David wrote the 139th Psalm. It is a psalm that reflects David's understanding of his uniqueness and purpose in God's economy.

In the psalm David recognizes that he is "fearfully and wonderfully made" (verse 14). He also acknowledges that God is the designer and creator of David's "inmost being" (verse 13). David is referring here to what we would call personality. David goes on to remark that his "unformed body" was not hidden from God, who "knit me together in my mother's womb" (verses 13-16). Finally, David reflects on the fact that all his days were written in God's book before one of them even transpired (verse 16).

If you put these observations together, you will see that David had a sense of God's providential control over the development of his physical body, his personality, and his life experience. All these factors worked together to create David's passion. He was designed to lead the people of Israel in paths of righteousness like a shepherd leads his flock. His passion was to be a godly leader. His gifts, life experience, and passion perfectly fit God's call on his life to be the king of Israel.

Like David, you are "custom-made" to accomplish God's purposes. The Apostle Paul tells us that we are God's "workmanship" and that we have been created to accomplish good works which God has prepared in advance for us to do (Ephesians 2:10). What a great picture! God prepares the work of peacemaking. God then designs and creates the peacemaker. God gifts the peacemaker with the abilities required to accomplish the work of peacemaking and then creates a passion in the peacemaker's heart to see the work done. God places a call on the peacemaker to do the work of peacemaking. Finally, God empowers the peacemaking enterprise with the enabling ability of His Spirit. When properly understood and experienced, peacemaking is a no-lose proposition. Every step of the way it is an "I can't, He can" operation!

Discerning the Call

Perhaps no dynamic of serving Christ is more complex and yet more simple than discerning the call of God. If you have never sensed God's call on your life, it is extremely complex to attempt to describe this mystical phenomenon. Once you have experienced a sense of call, the phenomenon is so simple it requires no explanation.

At times God actually gives a call to service in an audible voice. This was true of the prophet Samuel at the time of Eli (1 Samuel 3:1-10). Usually, the call is not audible but internal. God engineers the circumstances of our life in such a way that we are exposed to the need which will become our call. Having been exposed to the need, we begin to have an inner stirring to see something done about the situation. That inner stirring begins to grow in our life. We finally sense that we are the one to do something. Somewhere deep inside we know it is God who is prompting us. Someone has said that there are some things that you just "know in your knower."

When the call fits with our passion and our spiritual gifts, we can have confidence that we have found a place in which to be a peacemaker. We then must take action to serve our fellowman in the special arena God has designed for us. The result of our attempt will be a sense of God's blessing in our lives. We will see how God can use our lives to improve the quality of another person's life. This act of serving will lead to others. We will begin to become peacemakers. Our peacemaking efforts will begin to give our lives a new sense of purpose. We will be men who walk with Christ and make a difference in the world by being a servant of the Kingdom of God. We become men of action who are witnesses for Christ in our homes, our neighborhoods, our workplaces, and the world.

By this point in the book you might be feeling a bit

overwhelmed about how all the steps fit together. In the next chapter we will move into the laboratory of life and see what it might look like in the life of a man like yourself who learns to follow Christ, step by step.

CHECKPOINTS

Personal Reflection
1. What are you doing in your life that gives you true joy?
2. Do you love people, or do you love things?
3. How could you become a more effective witness?

Group Discussion
1. What needs in your church or community capture your interest?
2. Share what you think might be God's call on your life.
3. Discuss what your group could do as an act of service. Do it.

8
WORKING THE PROGRAM

A DAY IN THE LIFE

5:45 a.m.

Steve could hear a faint noise in the distance. He was sure he had heard it somewhere before, but was having a hard time remembering what it was. As a matter of fact, he seemed to be having a hard time remembering anything at all. His mind was a bit fuzzy. It seemed like only a minute ago that the checkered flag had dropped as he roared past the finish line to win Team Porsche's first Indy 500. Suddenly, the proper synapse fired and he remembered what the sound was: his alarm clock!

Coming into a state of mild consciousness, Steve reached over and shut off the alarm. As his eyes focused he read the numbers on the digital clock: 5:45. His first conscious thought was, *Surely, this must be a mistake!* Then the second enlightening memory of this fresh day materialized: he actually had set the clock for this time! Steve's normal wake-up time was 6:15, but this morning

131

was more than the first day of the rest of his life. This was the morning he had resolved to begin to become God's man. He was up a half hour early to review the seven steps and to put as many of them into action as he could before heading off to work.

Stumbling down the stairs, he thought of the events that had led to his early wake-up call. Two weeks before, he had attended the National Men's Conference in Boulder, Colorado. His good friend Rich had invited him to the event. Steve had made it clear that he was pretty ambivalent about church-type stuff. Rich had assured him that this would be different, and he was right.

A group of nearly fifty thousand men had filled Folsom Field at the University of Colorado. They were singing, shouting, giving each other high fives, and having the best time Steve had ever seen a bunch of men have in a football stadium where there wasn't a team on the field.

During the weekend, Steve understood for the first time the difference between religion and authentic Christianity. No wonder church had been so boring! He never had a clue about having a relationship with the living Christ. By the end of the time in Boulder, Steve had received Christ and had made the decision to try to be the kind of man he heard spoken of at the conference. Steve went home with motivation but without a clue of how to make that happen. When he told his buddy Rich how he was feeling, Rich performed the second act of true friendship in Steve's life. He gave him a book and told him to read it. The book: *Daily Disciplines for the Christian Man.*

Steve wasn't a big reader. He actually couldn't remember the last time he read a nonfiction book. After reading the first few pages of *Daily Disciplines*, Steve knew that this was a book he not only needed to read, but to put into practice. As a result, here he was, stumbling down the stairs at 5:45 in the morning to have his first time of working the program.

When he reached the bottom of the stairs, the thought passed through his mind, *I can't do this!* Before he had the chance to get discouraged by this thought, another came screaming into his consciousness: *Exactly!* Steve began to grin. Without even thinking about it he had just taken step one. Remembering the "I can't" illustration from the book, Steve thought to himself, *This is amazing! It's 5:45 in the morning and already I'm off to a good start.* By the time he reached the coffee maker there was a bounce in his step.

Settling into the chair now designated his own "prayer chair," Steve took a sip of coffee and said a quick prayer:

> *Lord, I really can't do this. Thank You that my inability to pull this off frees You to work in my life in a mighty way. Help me this morning because I've never done this before.*

Picking up the modern translation of the Bible his friend had helped him pick out, Steve turned to the inside cover where he had taped the tear-out appendix from *Daily Disciplines.* This was the page which contained a summary of the seven steps. There in black and white was the confirmation that he had correctly remembered step one:

> *STEP ONE – Acknowledging Our Need*
> *Father, I am spiritually powerless, and apart from Your divine intervention in my life I do not have the ability to be Your man (John 15:5).*

Glancing down to the next step, Steve again began to grin. This was the step affirming the truth that in the midst of his powerlessness, Christ had all the power necessary for Steve to be the man God wanted him to be on this day. He read:

STEP TWO – Affirming God's Power
Father, you are all-powerful. Only You have the ability
to enable me to become Your man (Philippians 4:13).

The very thought of being God's man was foreign to Steve. He always liked to think of himself as a normal guy, or at best a man's man. His image of what a godly man might look like had radically changed in the last two weeks. He now found himself actually desiring to become one. God's man—this was what he wanted to be; this was what he was designed and created to be. He knew that only God had the power to help him become one. Steve prayed again:

Lord, I agree with the truth of this second step. I know
that what I could never do, You can do. I'd like to be
Your man and do the things that would be pleasing to
You today.

This prayer took Steve right into the third step. He knew God had the power. Now he wanted to begin to tap into it. Looking down, he read the words of step three:

STEP THREE – Tapping into the Power
Holy Spirit, I need You to fill my life today with Your
presence and power. Live the life of Christ in and
through me today (Ephesians 5:18).

Steve had heard people talk about the Holy Spirit before. He found the subject very confusing, even after asking Christ into his life. In reading *Daily Disciplines* he started to understand how critically important the ministry of the Holy Spirit is in the daily life of a man who wants to follow Christ. He didn't understand it all, but he knew that the way Christ lived in him was by the presence of the Holy Spirit.

Steve found it very helpful to think of the illustration of the throne of his life. He wanted Christ to be on that throne. He knew that whatever else it meant to be "filled" with the Holy Spirit, this was at the heart of the matter. It was time to give this step a shot. Steve prayed once again:

> *Lord Jesus, take control of my life today. I want to live for You. Fill me with the presence and power of the Holy Spirit. I invite You to sit on the throne of my life today.*

6:00 a.m. — Coffee Break

By the time Steve got to this point in his quiet time, he was ready for another cup of coffee. Upon returning to his chair he decided to spend some time reading his Bible. Although this part of his program was found under step six, he didn't have need of steps four and five at the moment. He sensed that those were steps that would come in handy as he left the sheltered environment of home and headed off for a day in the urban "jungle."

Step six involved a commitment to grow in his relationship with Christ. It required the practice of the various basic disciplines of Christian growth. Steve actually began taking step six the minute he set his alarm the night before. He was up early to spend time reading his Bible and praying. This very thought passed through his mind as he looked down and read the words of the step:

> *STEP SIX – Growing in Christ*
> *I will seek through prayer, Bible study, and fellow-*
> *ship to improve my relationship with Christ. On a*
> *daily basis I will seek to know and do the will of God*
> *(1 Peter 2:2).*

Not really knowing how to tackle this big book called the Bible, Steve had asked a buddy where to start. His friend had suggested reading one chapter of Psalms a day, starting at the beginning. Since there are 150 chapters in the book of Psalms, he would read through the book once every five months. Since today was his first day, Steve turned to Psalm 1 to begin this discipline.

The psalm started with the words, "Blessed is the man." Even though Steve had never read this psalm before, he had a sense that this was a message for him. Deep inside he sensed that someone was telling him that he was going to be blessed if he did what this psalm said. Steve didn't know what to make of this inner sensation. Could this be what the book had talked about when it said God actually communicated with us through the Bible?

He read on:

> Blessed is the man
>   who does not walk in the counsel of the
>   wicked. . . .
> But his delight is in the law of the LORD.

Steve thought about this statement for a few moments. All his life he had listened to the voice of contemporary culture to develop his values and priorities. This approach to life must be what the psalmist called the "counsel of the wicked." Now he found himself getting up at 5:45 in the morning to "delight in" the law of the Lord. The thought seemed utterly amazing. This was good stuff!

After reading through the rest of the psalm in much the same way, Steve decided he would try to spend a few minutes praying. He had written down the outline of the Lord's Prayer as suggested in the book. Today he simply slowly prayed through each of the seven categories. As he prayed he was aware of the significance of each area and decided tomorrow to make a few notes about specific items he needed and wanted to pray about.

When he finished praying he looked at his watch. It was 6:15. Time to hit the shower and head to work.

7:00 a.m. — The Drive to Work
Driving to the office was always a challenging task. It was not unusual to spend a great deal of the trip down the freeway with a knot in his stomach. Mondays were hard days at work, and the freeway atmosphere reflected the fact that he was not the only one who felt like this. This morning, however, Steve found himself humming as he headed to the office. *This is really great!*, he thought to himself. It certainly wasn't the thought of going to work that was making him glad; it was the sense that he had been, and was, in fellowship with Christ.

Suddenly, a car pulled into the lane immediately behind his car and blasted its horn. The moment of peaceful reverie came to an abrupt end. Looking in the rearview mirror, he could see the angry face of the driver behind him. Steve was skilled at responding to these situations. An immediate tug-of-war commenced internally. Up until this very moment Steve knew that this morning he had allowed Christ to sit on that throne the book had talked about. Now he felt his ego battling to take back the throne and dictate his response to the driver in the mirror. In an instant a decision had to be made.

No! I'm not taking over. Christ, You stay in charge here, Steve prayed. He looked in the mirror and smiled. Graciously, he waved at the driver behind him. In response, the driver made his own not-so-gracious gesture. There were many days when this scenario would have had Steve out of his car and in the other driver's face. Instead, he found himself stunned and then amused. Christ was in control, and it was a much better feeling than letting ego usurp that inner throne.

8:00 a.m. — The Office

For most men our work is one of the primary arenas in which we are called to live out our Christian lives. Some men have the faulty mind-set that when you "punch in" for work you can "punch out" with Christ. Steve was nervous about how this new walk would play itself out at the office.

I have made a conscious decision not to tell you what Steve does for a living. I made this decision because I didn't want you to discount any of his experiences as irrelevant for you because you think your work is fundamentally different from his. For today, Steve is Everyman. His struggles are your struggles. His victories are your potential victories. If your "office" is a truck or a construction site, the challenges will be remarkably similar. Let's see how Steve handles them.

Arriving at the office, Steve encountered two immediate challenges to his walk. The first was Ruth Miller. Ms. Miller had been his boss's personal secretary since just after the first Ice Age. She was the first person you encountered walking through the office door, and it was always an unpleasant experience. The expression on her face as she monitored the incoming employees gave him the sensation of fingernails being scraped across a blackboard. Could Christ handle Ms. Miller?

Steve usually walked past without even acknowledging her presence. This subtle insult had been cultivated years ago. Entering the office he saw it: the look. This morning he walked right up to Ruth's desk, stopped, smiled, and said, "Good morning, Ruth." He walked on without even turning to see the astonished look on her face. Obstacle number one: handled with grace.

The next challenge would not be so easy. He had been thinking about Shirl on his drive to work. Before the past weekend he had enjoyed thinking about her in a not-so-wholesome way. Shirl was a total fox! She had come to work six months ago as a data processor. Her desk was on the way to his office and he ran into her frequently throughout the day. Although he had never cheated on his wife, the thought had crossed his mind a million times. Recently, most of those thoughts had been about Shirl.

During the men's conference the Holy Spirit had convicted him about his mental adultery. He had confessed and repented. He knew that the way he was fantasizing about Shirl was not helping his relationship with his wife. He had made a commitment at the conference to fidelity — not only outward fidelity, but fidelity of mind and spirit. The moment of testing had arrived.

Approaching Shirl's desk Steve prayed, *Lord, help me do this right*. He smiled and said, "Good morning, Shirl." He also remembered the verse his buddy gave him to memorize about this particular male struggle: "I made a covenant with my eyes not to look lustfully at a girl" (Job 31:1). He suddenly knew he had been looking at Shirl, and many other women, as objects instead of people. He had heard that language used before, but now he understood what it meant. As he headed for his office he said a short prayer for Shirl and asked God to bless her this day. Obstacle number two: mission accomplished.

10:30 — The Meeting

Monday mornings contained one element of his job that Steve was not particularly fond of: staff meetings. His preferred M.O. was to get into the office and dive into the work at hand. Although he knew meetings were important for the overall objectives of the company, he still found them to be frustrating and at times counterproductive. Part of his frustration stemmed from the fact that he really didn't care for a few of his colleagues.

The staff meeting began with a degree of predictability. Frank Slade, the president and CEO of the company, gave a brief pep talk about the status of the company and the pressing needs of the coming week. He then went around the table and asked each department head to give a brief update on his or her particular area of responsibility. The meeting went along fine until it came time for Dick Smith to report.

Dick was on a different wavelength than Steve. There was also a certain degree of healthy competition between the various departments that at times degenerated into an unhealthy envy. Dick and Steve had been through several tough encounters relating to their various areas of responsibility. Steve was totally unprepared for what was about to happen.

"I'd like to put a difficult issue on the table this morning," Dick began.

"Go ahead, Dick," Frank replied.

"Several of us have been concerned lately about the amount of attention and energy that are being spent on one of the departments at the expense of the rest of the business. We feel like Steve is getting a little out of control. Even though his department is performing well on paper, we feel that his attitude and aggressive nature are impairing our ability to accomplish our departmental objectives."

Steve sat stunned. He had just been ambushed by the one man sitting at the table who desperately wanted his job. Dick's area was one of the weakest in the company, and his one of the strongest. Now Dick was blaming his poor results on Steve. Something inside began to heat up.

"We are supposed to be a team," Dick continued. "How can we be a team if one or two prima donnas are allowed to use an inordinate amount of the company's resources to make themselves look good while the rest of us attempt to do our jobs with one hand tied behind our backs? It is time someone put a stop to this for the sake of the company."

The words cut like a knife. "Prima donna . . . inordinate resources . . . make themselves look good." The inner heat reached the boiling point and the flesh jumped up and dethroned Christ. Before he even knew what happened, the words came gushing out of Steve's mouth: "You little incompetent [expletive deleted]! If you put as much energy into doing your job as you do into kissing Frank's [expletive deleted], your department would be performing as well as mine!"

It all happened before he knew what hit him. Amazingly, as he looked around the table, no one else even seemed fazed. Then it dawned on him: this was the way he always talked. To the men and women sitting in the room, nothing had changed. But Steve knew otherwise. He had been walking with Christ all weekend. The morning had started off great as he walked in the Spirit. During the meeting, however, he knew who was occupying the throne of his life. He had just moved full speed into the flesh.

Noon—Lunch Time
The rest of the staff meeting went without incident. Dick had responded to Steve's attack with his wounded puppy routine. The meeting adjourned and Steve headed back to his office. Looking at his schedule, he was glad to see that the lunch hour was free. He needed it. He buzzed his secretary and told her he would be gone for an hour and a half at lunch.

There was a quiet park with a great mountain view not far from the office. Steve walked to a remote part of the park and sat down with his back against a tree and the mountains in plain sight. What went wrong? He prayed, *Lord, I know I fouled it up and I'm not even sure what happened. I'd like to work through this and get back on track, but I don't have the ability to do it.* Deep inside a definite impression drifted into his consciousness. It seemed to communicate the affirmation, "Exactly!"

Back to step one. Steve remembered, "I can't! I am powerless over the effects of my separation from God. Apart from His intervention I don't have a chance." Quickly he moved into steps two and three. *Lord, You can! You have the ability to get me back on track. Holy Spirit, I don't fully understand what all this means, but I invite You to fill my life again.*

Opening the cover of his Bible, Steve glanced down the quick reference guide to the steps. Now he needed steps four and five. He actually felt like he needed step five before step four. It was obvious that along with getting back into the flesh, he had violated God's law in attitude, action, and intent. He needed to tap into the cleansing power of Christ. He read the words of step five:

STEP FIVE – Experiencing Spiritual Cleansing
Lord Jesus, I am a sinner constantly in need of Your
grace and the experience of Your forgiveness. Help me
be honest with You today. I will confess, repent, and
make restitution where appropriate (1 John 1:9).

Without knowing it Steve had developed a very
simple and effective approach to his new commitment
to Christ. He had come to believe in the inspiration
and authority of the Bible. In faith, if the Bible said it,
he believed it. This was especially helpful at this very
moment. The tendency of many men is to get hooked
into a subtle form of self-atonement by feeling guilty
and becoming spiritually immobilized after a failure like
Steve had experienced. Because of his faith, Steve simply
took the step and believed it.

Jesus, I am a sinner, he prayed. *Thank You that You died*
for me. Lifting his head, Steve looked at the mountains
in the distance. Out of nowhere came the words into
his mind, "I will lift up my eyes to the mountains." He
knew it was somewhere in the Bible, but at the moment
he simply remembered the next words, "From where my
help comes." He had the sense God was speaking to him
through the Word.

Lord, I specifically confess my blowup as sin. Not only
was what I did wrong, but I know I took over the lord-
ship of my life in a split second. Thank You for Your
forgiveness. Thank You that when You died on the cross
You paid the price for what happened in that meeting.
Cleanse me, Lord.

With step five appropriated Steve turned his attention to step four. He read the words of the step:

STEP FOUR – Maintaining Christ's Lordship
Lord Jesus, I willingly relinquish the throne of my life
and invite You to once again take control as Lord of my
life (1 Peter 3:15).

He had drawn the throne illustrations from *Daily Disciplines* on his seven-step summary page. Steve knew the probabilities were high that he would need these tools repeatedly. There was no doubt which circle the blowup put him in. There also was no doubt which circle he wanted to represent his life. Once more, in faith, Steve prayed, *Lord Jesus, I have moved You off the throne of my life by my sin. I willingly step down from the throne and invite You to rule and reign again in my life. Live Your life in and through me this afternoon.*

Steve walked into that park living in the defeat of the old man. He walked out in the grace of Christ, back in the reality of the new man. With caution, and with a sense of gratitude, he headed back to the office.

2:00 p.m. – The Afternoon
The afternoon went well. For most of the time the work of the day kept him occupied. Losing Monday mornings to staff meetings always put pressure on Monday afternoons. As he worked he began to have a gnawing sense that there was something he had forgotten or needed to do. As far as he could tell, all of the steps were in place and Christ was firmly enthroned as Lord. As the afternoon wore on the internal discomfort grew. *Lord, what is going on? Is there something I forgot?* he prayed silently.

No sooner had this subvocal prayer been expressed than he had a sudden need to go to the washroom. On the way he passed Dick's office. A clear sense of conviction penetrated all defense systems. This was it. He had confessed, repented, and asked Christ to take over. What he had failed to think through was the issue of restitution. He had unfinished business with Dick.

Knocking on Dick's door was one of the hardest steps of obedience he had taken. At a feeling level he did not want to do this. Deep down he knew he had to.

"Come in," the voice inside the office said.

The look on Dick's face was one of surprise and suspicion. As far as he could remember, Steve didn't think he had ever been in Dick's office.

"Could I talk with you for a minute?" Steve asked with a gentle voice.

"Have a seat," Dick offered, still looking wary.

Inside, Steve was praying like crazy. *Help, Lord. Help! I can't, but You can.* "I'd like to talk with you about this morning," he calmly stated. "I was way out of line in what I said to you. I'd like to apologize and ask you to forgive me." Steve could hardly believe what he had just said. It was as spontaneous as the earlier insult, but this time the words came straight from the new nature instead of the old. He couldn't ever remember asking anyone to forgive him.

Dick sat dumbfounded. He didn't know how to respond. After a moment's pause he blurted out, "What's wrong with you?" It wasn't a well-thought-out question. It was a response coming from his own shock at what was taking place.

Steve laughed and the tension broke. "Nothing. I just came to grips with the fact that I acted like a jerk and needed to ask for your forgiveness."

"That isn't quite your style," Dick observed.

"Yeah, well, I'm hoping to change my style a bit." Suddenly, another impulse was stirring within. Steve had the impression that he was supposed to tell Dick about the conference and his new commitment to Christ. A series of words flashed through his mind: *Quadrant Four invading Quadrant Three . . . Ministry! . . . Witness! . . . Dick? . . . No way! . . . Way!!!*

This was getting wild! Internally, a minor war was being waged. Steve was definitely being prompted to share his faith. Along with the prompting there was definite resistance. New words flashed across the inner screen: *Not Dick . . . What will he think? . . . What will he tell the other guys? . . . What will he tell the boss?*

As these thoughts raced through his brain he could feel his heart rate increase and the adrenaline begin to pump. Flight or fight. A choice had to be made. Steve was a fighter. God made him that way. He remembered: *Quadrant One resists ministry and witness. I'm going for it!*

"Dick, do you know anything about Jesus Christ?" He couldn't believe he said it, but the look on Dick's face made it all worthwhile.

"Well, sure. Who doesn't?" Dick responded with a bit of confusion.

"No, I mean, do you really know anything about Jesus, personally?" Steve asked.

"I'm not sure what you mean," Dick answered.

"I thought I knew about Jesus," Steve affirmed. "At least I used His name enough during the course of a day that you would have thought we were bosom buddies. But I found out recently that I didn't have a clue who Jesus was."

"I heard you went to some religious thing," Dick offered.

How did he know that? Steve wondered. "I don't know if I would call it a religious thing. I went to a men's conference and heard that Jesus wasn't even interested in religion," Steve continued.

"What do you mean?" Dick asked.

"I guess I always thought Christianity was a religion. I thought it was all about not doing all the things I was having fun doing. At the conference I learned that Christianity is supposed to be a relationship with the living God through Jesus Christ," Steve shared.

Dick's face looked blank. To Steve it appeared as if what he just said must have sounded like a foreign language to Dick. It began to feel like it was time to back off.

"Anyway, I didn't come in here to bore you with this. I really wanted to ask your forgiveness. Will you forgive me?" Steve asked.

"Sure," Dick replied. "After all, I was really a jerk, too."

"If you ever want to talk more about Christ, just say the word," Steve offered.

As he walked out of Dick's office he felt like a million dollars. He had just done two things he was totally unable to do in his own strength. He had made restitution with a man he had despised for years, and he had actually taken step seven. The words of the text which accompanied the step flashed through his mind: "And you will be My witnesses." He couldn't remember the reference, so he went immediately back to his office to look it up. He was so excited he even forgot to take a minute to check out how Shirl was looking.

Flipping open his Bible to the summary page, he read:

STEP SEVEN – Serving the Kingdom
Lord Jesus, by Your grace and with Your help I will seek to be Your witness in my home, in my neighborhood, in my workplace, and in the world. Live Your life through me today (Acts 1:8).

This was great! A seed had just been planted for the Kingdom of God. Steve stopped and silently prayed:

Lord, I pray for Dick. Use what was just said to begin to get him to think about You. Make me sensitive to know when to share more. Help me serve Dick in a way that will bring glory to You.

5:00 p.m. — Home for the Day

By the time Steve left for home he was feeling bushed. It had been an emotionally draining day with big ups and big downs. He had worked hard all afternoon to catch up on his work load. Normally, this was the time of day when he could go home and relax for a few hours before dinner.

He could see his son standing in the driveway as he pulled around the corner. Bobby was throwing a ball against the house and catching it with his ball glove. Pulling into the driveway, Steve remembered a line from the section of the book dealing with priorities. The line went something like "When I get home, I begin the most important work of the day."

He pulled in and looked in the face of his young son. Written all across it was the look of need. How had he been so blind? Day after day he came home, read the paper, looked through magazines, and watched television while his son was neglected. *Forgive me, Lord. I have been a fool.*

As soon as the car was parked in the garage he went back outside. "Bobby! Let's play catch," he said with great enthusiasm. The look on his son's face was worth a million dollars.

"Do you mean it, Dad?" Bobby asked.

The words cut to his heart. His own son couldn't even believe his dad would take the time to play catch.

"Absolutely, Son!"

A few minutes later Steve's wife, Grace, opened the door and looked out to find out what was wrong. She had heard the car pull into the garage and she knew her husband's afternoon routine. When she saw the boys playing catch, and the look on her son's face, she began to get teary-eyed. Something was happening to Steve and it was good.

7:00 p.m. – An Evening at Home

Dinner was chaotic but fun. Steve told Grace and the kids the stories about his first day attempting to implement the seven steps. Grace didn't know whether to laugh or cry as he shared the story about Dick. She had seen Shirl on her visits to the office and was nervous about having such an attractive woman in daily contact with her husband. Steve's honesty and desire to have the right attitude gave her great relief. The interaction between the two was good. Steve sensed something was different.

Something was different about the kids, too. He couldn't put his finger on it, but the whole family seemed more cohesive. After dinner Grace and he went for a walk together. They talked about their relationship and what they could do to make it more of a priority. They talked and laughed and enjoyed each other more than they had in many months. Grace encouraged him about the changes she could see in him since the weekend conference. She also asked if a woman could read *Daily Disciplines for the Christian Man*. Steve jokingly assured her it would probably not radically impact her sexuality if she did. He also told her he thought she would find it as helpful as he did.

After the walk Steve and Grace started the nightly task of getting the kids ready for bed. Steve was determined to use this time to begin giving his children the spiritual leadership he had neglected over the years. He had sent them to Sunday school while he stayed home and watched ball games on television, but he knew now that part of what it meant to be God's man involved taking the lead in the spiritual nurture of his family.

He called Sarah to come join him in Bobby's room. When the two children were together he asked, "How would you like me to read you a story tonight?"

"Yeah!" the children exclaimed in unison.

With fear and trepidation Steve read a chapter out of John's gospel from the version of the Bible the children had been given at Sunday school. When he was finished he sent Sarah back to her room with the assurance he would be in to pray for her. Then he knelt by the side of Bobby's bed, placed his hand on his son, and prayed for him. When he was finished he went to Sarah's room and did the same for her. It seemed like a small step, but something about this time with his children gave him a deep sense of personal satisfaction.

With the kids in bed the house quieted down significantly. Thinking through the events of the day, Steve had a sense that this had been a very important day in his life. He had used the spiritual principles contained in the seven steps to put the commitments he made at the men's conference into action in his daily life. Things had gone well. Even the blowup at work had been used to teach him important realities about the spiritual life. He had found a program that worked, and he had worked the program.

10:30 p.m. — Bedtime

Climbing into bed, Steve leaned over and kissed Grace goodnight. She smiled in her semiconscious state. He leaned back against his pillow and thought through the events of the day one last time. Could he live consistently like this? He wasn't sure. It sure was worth giving it his best shot though! What had been the key? As he thought through all that had happened, he could see the hand of Christ at work in him and through him. That was always the key: "I can't, He can!" "How true," Steve reflected.

He looked over at the clock. The alarm was set for 5:45 a.m. Steve reached over and grabbed the clock. He saw the button marked "Alarm Set." With a smile on his face he reset the alarm . . . for 5:40 a.m. He turned off the lights and drifted off to sleep with thoughts of winning the Indy 500 returning to his dreams.

THE SEVEN STEPS

Step One — Acknowledging Our Need
Father, I am spiritually powerless, and apart from Your divine intervention in my life I do not have the ability to be Your man (John 15:5).

Step Two — Affirming God's Power
Father, You are all-powerful. Only You have the ability to enable me to become Your man (Philippians 4:13).

Step Three — Tapping into the Power
Holy Spirit, I need You to fill my life today with Your presence and power. Live the life of Christ in and through me today (Ephesians 5:18).

Step Four — Maintaining Christ's Lordship
Lord Jesus, I willingly relinquish the throne of my life and invite You to once again take control as Lord of my life (1 Peter 3:15).

Step Five — Experiencing Spiritual Cleansing
Lord Jesus, I am a sinner constantly in need of Your grace and the experience of Your forgiveness. Help me be honest with You today. I will confess, repent, and make restitution where appropriate (1 John 1:9).

Step Six — Growing in Christ
I will seek through prayer, Bible study, and fellowship to improve my relationship with Christ. On a daily basis I will seek to know and do the will of God (1 Peter 2:2).

Step Seven — Serving the Kingdom
Lord Jesus, by Your grace and with Your help I will seek to be Your witness in my home, in my neighborhood, in my workplace, and in the world. Live Your life through me today (Acts 1:8).

AUTHOR

Bob Beltz is the executive pastor of Cherry Hills Community church in Englewood, Colorado. For the last ten years he has been part of the leadership team that has seen the church grow from a handful of men to one of the fastest growing churches in North America. Originally from Kansas City, Missouri, Bob and his wife, Allison, moved to Colorado in 1975 to attend Denver Conservative Baptist Seminary, where Bob earned both his Master of Arts and Doctor of Ministry degrees.

As executive pastor, Bob has been able to utilize his gifts in the areas of teaching and leadership. His Wednesday evening Bible study averages over one thousand men and women. On Tuesday mornings Bob teaches a men's Bible study attended by three hundred businessmen from the Denver community. For over ten years Bob has also served as an adjunct staff member of the Executive Network, helping businessmen grow in the areas of priorities and relationships.

Bob and Allison have two children: a daughter, Stephanie, and a son, Baker. Bob is also the author of *Transforming Your Prayer Life*, a guide to developing a more meaningful relationship with God, and *How to Survive the End of the World*, a layman's commentary on the book of Revelation.

THE SEVEN STEPS

Step One—Acknowledging Our Need
Father, I am spiritually powerless, and apart from Your divine intervention in my life I do not have the ability to be Your man (John 15:5).

Step Two—Affirming God's Power
Father, You are all-powerful. Only You have the ability to enable me to become Your man (Philippians 4:13).

Step Three—Tapping into the Power
Holy Spirit, I need You to fill my life today with Your presence and power. Live the life of Christ in and through me today (Ephesians 5:18).

Step Four—Maintaining Christ's Lordship
Lord Jesus, I willingly relinquish the throne of my life and invite You to once again take control as Lord of my life (1 Peter 3:15).

Step Five—Experiencing Spiritual Cleansing
Lord Jesus, I am a sinner constantly in need of Your grace and the experience of Your forgiveness. Help me be honest with You today. I will confess, repent, and make restitution where appropriate (1 John 1:9).

Step Six—Growing in Christ
I will seek through prayer, Bible study, and fellowship to improve my relationship with Christ. On a daily basis I will seek to know and do the will of God (1 Peter 2:2).

Step Seven—Serving the Kingdom
Lord Jesus, by Your grace and with Your help I will seek to be Your witness in my home, in my neighborhood, in my workplace, and in the world. Live Your life through me today (Acts 1:8).